THE BEST OF **W**OODWORKER'S **J**OURNAL

Benches, Chairs & Beds

Practical Projects from Shaker to Contemporary

THE BEST OF **Woodworker's Journal**

Benches, Chairs & Beds

Practical Projects from Shaker to Contemporary

from the editors of *Woodworker's Journal*

Fox Chapel Publishing

1970 Broad Street • East Petersburg, PA 17520
www.FoxChapelPublishing.com

Compilation Copyright © 2007 by Fox Chapel Publishing Company, Inc.

Text and Illustration Copyright © 2007 by *Woodworker's Journal. Woodworker's Journal* is a publication of Rockler Press.

Benches, Chairs & Beds: Practical Projects from Shaker to Contemporary is a compilation first published in 2007 by Fox Chapel Publishing Company, Inc. The patterns contained herein are copyrighted by *Woodworker's Journal*.

Our friends at Rockler Woodworking and Hardware supplied us with most of the hardware used in this book. Visit *rockler.com*. For subscription information to *Woodworker's Journal* magazine, call toll-free 1-800-765-4119 or visit *www.woodworkersjournal.com*.

Fox Chapel Publishing Company, Inc.
President: Alan Giagnocavo
Publisher: J. McCrary
Acquisition Editor: Peg Couch
Editor: Gretchen Bacon
Associate Editor: Patty Sinnott
Series Editor: John Kelsey
Creative Direction: Troy Thorne
Cover Design: Lindsay Hess

Woodworker's Journal
Publisher: Ann Rockler Jackson
Editor-in-Chief: Larry N. Stoiaken
Editor: Rob Johnstone
Art Director: Jeff Jacobson
Senior Editor: Joanna Werch Takes
Field Editor: Chris Marshall
Illustrators: Jeff Jacobson, John Kelliher

ISBN 978-1-56523-343-0

Publisher's Cataloging-in-Publication Data

Benches, chairs & beds : practical projects from Shaker to contemporary / from the editors of Woodworker's journal. -- East Petersburg, PA : Fox Chapel Publishing, c2007.

 p. ; cm.

 (The best of Woodworker's journal)

 ISBN: 978-1-56523-343-0

  1. Furniture making. 2. Furniture design. 3. Benches. 4. Chairs.
 5. Beds. 6. Woodwork--Patterns.
 I. Benches, chairs, and beds. II. Woodworker's journal.

TT194 .B46 2007
684.104--dc22   0710

To learn more about the other great books from Fox Chapel Publishing, or to find a retailer near you, call toll-free 1-800-457-9112 or visit us at *www.FoxChapelPublishing.com*.

Printed in China
10 9 8 7 6 5 4 3 2 1

Note to Authors: We are always looking for talented authors to write new books in our area of woodworking, design, and related crafts. Please send a brief letter describing your idea to Peg Couch, Acquisition Editor, Fox Chapel Publishing, 1970 Broad Street, East Petersburg, PA 17520.

Introduction

Some years back, contributing editor Mike McGlynn was building a Frank Lloyd Wright–inspired chair for *Woodworker's Journal*. I noticed that he had added some rails to the original design, and I asked why. "The underlying principle behind all my joinery choices is strength," he said. "No piece of furniture takes as much abuse as a chair. If you don't make it bombproof, it will soon become loose and fall apart." As usual, Mike was exactly right, and I think you'll find that all the chairs (and benches) that we selected for this book subscribe to his theory. Even Stephen Shepherd's ladder-back chair, which at first appears a little spindly, is as solid as can be.

We're featuring some real American classics in the chair section, from that ladder-back (popular at the turn of the nineteenth century in both Canada and the colonies) to the Van Pelts' classic Adirondack that incorporates design elements from the Greene brothers. We've also included a couple of designs that you don't see that often, such as Ralph Bagnall's Hoosier step stool (a midwestern classic) and Rick White's amazing portable folding chairs (one of them found a place right in my office!).

Chairs have to be bombproof, but outdoor benches have to weather storms, as well. We offer two beauties in this book: Chris Inman's classic white-oak English garden bench and Chris Marshall's imaginative hoop-back design, which relies on reclaimed cypress to fight the elements. And for the foyer,

we have three designs for you: Greg Wood's timber-framed split-mortise bench, Jim Jacobson's frame-and-panel entry bench, and Chris Inman's unbelievable New England settle. I well recall lugging the reclaimed heart pine for that project down to Chris' basement shop. The resin from that pine, probably more than 200 years old, really put his blades to the test!

And finally … beds. Our own shop master, Rick White, built three of the offerings here, each as unique as you could ask for! I particularly like his Murphy bed, as did many of our readers when this project first appeared. Chris Inman turned things back toward a more traditional look with his classic bed frame design, and new woodworker LiLi Jackson built a classic pencil post bed that is both elegant and sturdy.

With so many projects to choose from, you're sure to find plenty to keep you busy in your shop. So, turn the page and get started!

Larry N. Stoiaken, Editor-in-Chief

Acknowledgments

Woodworker's Journal recently celebrated its 30th anniversary—a benchmark few magazines ever reach. I would like to acknowledge both the 300,000 woodworkers who make up our readership and Rockler Woodworking and Hardware (*rockler.com*), which provided most of the hardware, wood, and other products used to build the projects in this book. Our publishing partner, Fox Chapel, did a terrific job re-presenting our material, and I am especially grateful to Alan Giagnocavo, Gretchen Bacon, John Kelsey, and Troy Thorne for their commitment to our content.

Larry N. Stoiaken, Editor-in-Chief

Contents

Beds 109

119

Benches

Split-Mortise Bench

Timber-framed joinery in a 100-year-old smokehouse provided the inspiration for the split-cut mortises on this sturdy bench. The rest of the styling is straightforward and can be reproduced with a band saw and a drum sander. A dash of contrasting wood in the seat and the stretcher adds a bit of flair.

by Greg Wood

There's something special about mortise-and-tenon joinery. Lots of woodworkers feel dovetails are more romantic, but when I stand in my 100-year-old smokehouse, especially during one of our infamous Minnesota snowstorms, the immense strength of the structure's mortise-and-tenon joinery quite reassures me.

The pegged timber-frame joints in the building were, in part, the inspiration for this bench. Though the design is simple, its execution may be a little more demanding than it looks. For example, there are some tight tolerances on the pegged-tenon joints that hold the stretcher to the legs. And the leg tops are angled slightly to make the seat more comfortable.

I've always believed that fine craftsmanship should be so in tune with design that it takes a while to notice that you're looking at something special. That's what I'd like you to experience when building this bench.

Choosing a Wood Species

I chose hard maple for this bench because its understated grain and texture complement the simple lines of the design. In addition, the bench should appear sturdy and functional—hence, the thick stock used throughout. If you have difficulty finding 1½"-thick material, face gluing ¾" boards together will work equally well. If you choose to go the latter route, make sure the figure patterns along the edges are fairly similar,

Figure 1: *The split mortise in each leg is created by ripping stock down the center, dadoing half the mortise out of each piece (shown here), and then regluing the two pieces.*

because visible joints may detract from the finished piece. Also, to prevent voids in the glued-up panel, use clamps with long jaws, and start clamping from the center out.

Once you've settled on your wood species, it's a good idea to store the stock in your workshop for a week or two, just to let it acclimate. With the precise tenons you'll be milling, it's better that you don't have to deal with too much shrinkage or expansion. Also, cut all the parts ⅛" oversize, and then wait another week before jointing them to the exact dimensions in the Material List on page 5.

Making Mortises the Easy Way

When I started this project, I figured that the biggest challenge would be making the large through mortise in each leg (pieces 1). With visions of sharp chisels cracking the 1½"-thick hard maple along its grain, I began searching for a better method than drill-and-chisel. What I came up with was a technique appropriately borrowed from timber framers. I simply ripped each leg's middle board down the center, removed half the mortise from each side using a dado blade on the table saw (see Figure 1 on page 3), and reglued the board.

Each of these reassembled middle pieces then became the center of a 16⅝"-wide panel, which in turn served as the blank from which the leg was cut (see the leg pattern on page 7). Again, pay attention to the grain pattern, because matching grains help make a panel look seamless. Use dowels or biscuits to keep the parts aligned, and apply enough clamping pressure to close the joint tight, but not so much that you squeeze out too much glue.

Figure 2: *To define the stretcher tenons, use a sharp, fine-toothed blade, and then reveal the cheeks with a dado set.*

Figure 3: *Dry fit the stretcher in the leg mortises to ensure a perfect fit.*

Stretcher Tenon Detail

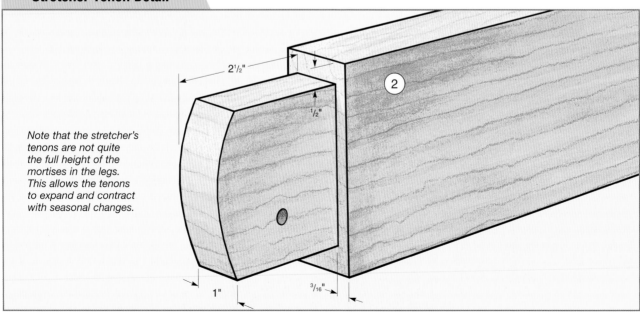

Note that the stretcher's tenons are not quite the full height of the mortises in the legs. This allows the tenons to expand and contract with seasonal changes.

2½"

½"

②

1"

3/16"

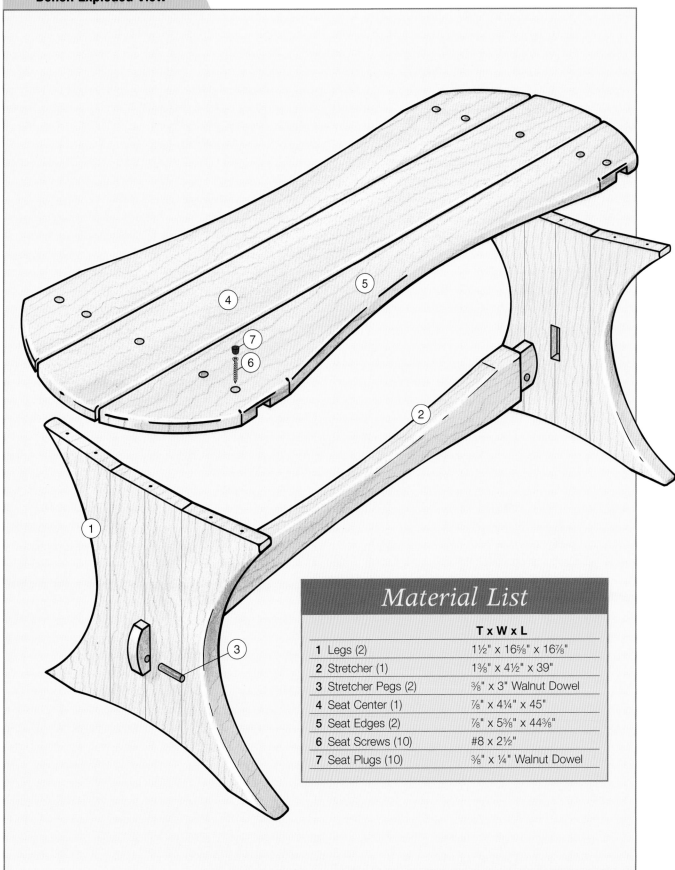

Material List

		T x W x L
1	Legs (2)	1½" x 16⅝" x 16⅞"
2	Stretcher (1)	1⅜" x 4½" x 39"
3	Stretcher Pegs (2)	⅜" x 3" Walnut Dowel
4	Seat Center (1)	⅞" x 4¼" x 45"
5	Seat Edges (2)	⅞" x 5⅝" x 44⅜"
6	Seat Screws (10)	#8 x 2½"
7	Seat Plugs (10)	⅜" x ¼" Walnut Dowel

Figure 4: *Most of the edges of the split-mortise bench are rounded over with different bits before final assembly.*

When the glue cures, temporarily attach a copy of the pattern to one face of each panel (use double-sided tape or spray-mount adhesive), and carefully cut just outside the lines with your band saw. Then, using a drum sander in your drill press or an oscillating spindle sander, sand it up to the lines.

Making the Pegged-Tenon Stretcher

Any pro will tell you that, when milling several operations on a single part, start with the most difficult one. That way, if you make a mistake, you'll only be out a board, instead of a board and a lot of time.

The most demanding cuts on the stretcher (piece 2) are the tenons on the ends. Begin by laying out these tenons, as shown in the stretcher tenon detail drawing on page 4. Note that the tenons are not quite the full height of the mortises you've already cut in the legs. This is because wood moves more across the grain than along it, and the tongues must be allowed to expand and contract widthwise.

The best way to form the tenons is to use a tenoning jig, but an accurately set miter gauge will also work for cutting the tenons facedown. If you opt for the miter gauge, attach an auxiliary extension fence to its face to support this long workpiece.

Define the cheeks and shoulders with a sharp, fine-toothed blade, and then switch to a dado blade to remove the waste (see Figure 2 on page 4). Use scrap wood to establish the correct blade height before cutting into your workpiece.

Dry fit each tenon in its respective mortise (see Figure 3 on page 4), and mark the hole locations for the stretcher pegs (pieces 3). Drill a ⅜" hole for each peg, using your drill press to ensure a 90° hole (see the stretcher pattern on page 7 for the peg hole location). Then, fashion the pegs by cutting them to

length and easing the ends with your belt sander. Test the fit by installing the pegs in your leg-and-stretcher assembly.

Remove the stretcher, and use your band saw and belt sander to create the gentle curves on the ends of the tenons, as well as the curved profile down the center of the stretcher (see the stretcher pattern). With that done, it's time to turn your attention to the seat boards.

Fashioning the Seat Boards

Ideally, the three seat boards (pieces 4 and 5) should be cut from a single wide board so their grain forms a pattern extending all the way across the seat. If that's not possible, find three boards that match well.

Use the seat patterns on page 7 to lay out the profile of each board, and then make all the straight cuts on your table saw. While the boards are still rectangular, cut dadoes in the underside of each where the legs will join the seat. Check your cuts by dry fitting each board to the legs as you go. Make the curved cuts on the seat edges with your band saw, finishing with a drum sander in the drill press. Now, use the patterns to locate the screw holes in the seat top. Turn the seat boards upside down, and center the ³⁄₁₆" pilot holes for attachment screws in the dadoes. Then, flip the boards over, and use a Forstner bit to create counterbores on the top for plugging the screw heads; use a drill press for boring these holes. Dry assemble the whole bench, and use a portable drill (switch to a ⅛" bit) to extend the pilot holes down into the tops of the legs.

Final Assembly and Finishing

Before final assembly, install a ⅜"-radius roundover bit in your router, and soften the legs (except their top edges) and the stretcher (except its tenons), as shown in Figure 4. Now, switch to a ¼"-radius roundover bit, and soften the seat boards (being cautious around the dadoes).

Glue and clamp the stretcher to the legs, wiping off any excess glue with a wet rag, and then tap the pegs into their holes. Now, line up your pilot holes, and attach the seat boards to the legs, using #8 flathead wood screws (pieces 6) instead of glue. Remember to check that your assembly is perfectly square as you go.

When everything has dried, make some face-grain seat plugs (pieces 7) from a contrasting wood that matches the pegs (I used walnut). Then, glue them into their counterbores, and sand the surfaces flush. Continue sanding everything down through the grits to 180, and wipe all the surfaces with a tack cloth before applying your favorite topcoat. For this rustic bench, a satin varnish or several coats of shellac will create a fitting low-luster sheen.

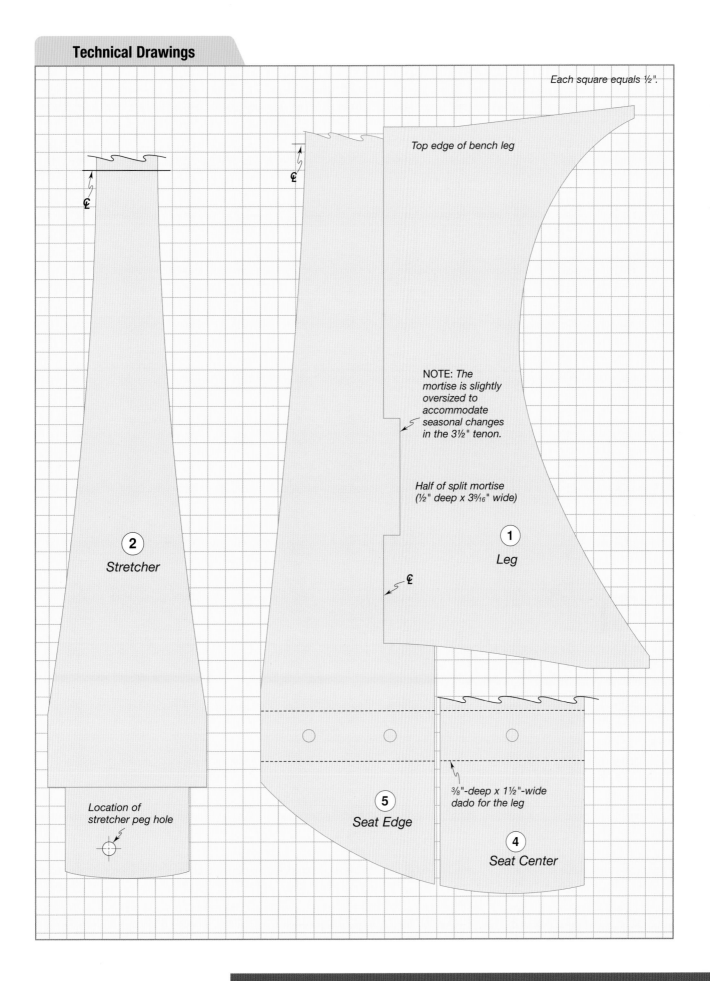

Each square equals ½".

Top edge of bench leg

NOTE: *The mortise is slightly oversized to accommodate seasonal changes in the 3½" tenon.*

Half of split mortise (½" deep x 3⁹⁄₁₆" wide)

①
Leg

②
Stretcher

Location of stretcher peg hole

⑤
Seat Edge

⅜"-deep x 1½"-wide dado for the leg

④
Seat Center

New England Settle

Equally fitting next to the fireplace or in the entryway, this colonial bench will warm your home with its old-world charm. To enhance the project's aged appearance, build it from reclaimed heart pine, the kind of wood our forefathers used.

by Chris Inman

In colonial times, homes were drafty places, and a roaring fire was the only means of taking the chill off a winter evening. To get the most out of that roaring fire, colonists often placed their settles in front of the fireplace. The high, solid backs acted like walls, effectively reducing the size of a room and concentrating the warm air in a smaller area. Even though the settle wasn't very comfortable, the premium on warmth made it the most popular seat in the house.

Of course, we have furnaces today, so settles aren't necessary. However, their sentimental warmth continues to make a room more inviting, and they can still serve a practical function. Near a hearth, a settle creates a cozy nook for reading, and its chest is ideal for storing a few extra logs. Placed near an entryway, a settle serves as a seat for changing boots and a chest for storing mittens, scarves, and hats. For a real treat, line the chest bottom with aromatic cedar, and use the settle in a bedroom to hold spare blankets.

Carpenters of the colonial era used heart pine for this type of project, a wood that is largely unavailable today. But with our limited wood resources, it has become economical to salvage lumber from deteriorating old buildings. The heart pine in this settle was once a warehouse beam, and the tree it came from was probably harvested in the mid-nineteenth century. If you like building reproductions of traditional country furniture, this is one of the best woods to choose, and there are numerous Internet suppliers of reclaimed heart pine.

Building the settle requires 72 board feet of ¾"-thick stock and 3 board feet of 3" x 2½" material. For some parts in the chest, you'll need 7 board feet of a secondary wood, such as poplar. The only hardware required is a 36" piano hinge. Plan on spending about 25 hours to build your settle.

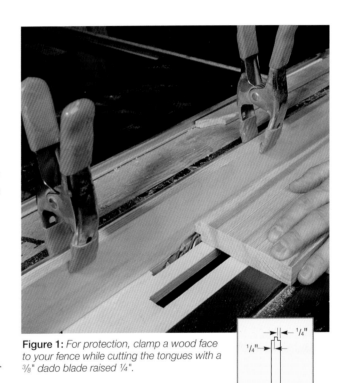

Figure 1: *For protection, clamp a wood face to your fence while cutting the tongues with a ⅜" dado blade raised ¼".*

Getting Underway

Start this project by making panels for the sides (pieces 1), seat (piece 2), and bottom (piece 3). Select nicely matched pine stock for the sides and seat, and use poplar for the bottom. Cut the boards a few inches longer than the lengths given in the Material List on page 13. Once you have the boards arranged, draw a big triangle across each panel to use as an alignment reference when gluing them together. Then, joint the boards, and glue up the panels, making sure to alternate the clamps to keep the panels flat. When the excess glue has set to a rubbery consistency, shear it off with a chisel.

Figure 3: *For the shiplaps, use a ¾" dado blade raised ⅜", and make the cuts with the help of your miter gauge. Keep the scrap wood face clamped to the rip fence during this operation.*

While your panels are drying, turn your attention to cutting the tongue-and-groove boards for the settle's back (pieces 4, 5, and 6) and front (pieces 7, 8, and 9). First, rip the stock to width, and then cut the pieces a little longer than their finished lengths. Since you're set up for ripping, cut stock for the crest rail (piece 10) and back rail (piece 11). Then, tilt your blade 30°, and bevel the top front edge of the back rail. Set these last two pieces aside for now.

On tongue-and-groove joints, it's best to form the grooves first and then cut the tongues to fit. Set up a ¼" dado blade in your table saw, raise it ⅜", and adjust your fence to center the blade on the edge of your pine stock. Set aside the boards for the left end of the bench (pieces 4 and 7), and then plow a groove into one edge of the others.

To cut the tongues, install a ⅜" dado blade and raise it ¼". Clamp a wood face to the fence for protection (see Figure 1 on page 9), and adjust the fence so the face barely touches the blade. Cut a tongue on some scrap pine, and test its fit in a groove. If the tongue slips in easily without sloppiness, the fit is perfect. Now, set the right-end stock aside (pieces 6 and 9), and cut tongues on the rest of the boards.

Cut all the boards to length, arrange them in order, and mark their front faces. All the back boards meet the crest rail with a shiplap joint rather than a tongue-and-groove joint (see Figure 2). In this situation, a shiplap is better because it leaves more material on the back side of

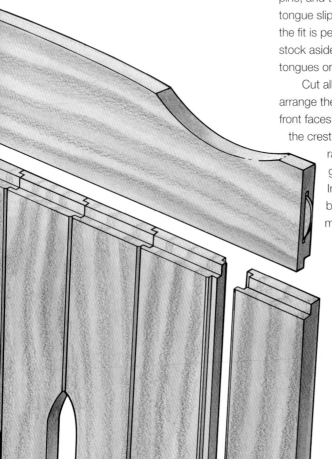

Figure 2: *This view from behind the settle shows the shiplap joints, as well as the tongue-and-groove joints between the boards. The crest rail should not be shaped until after the rabbet has been cut along its bottom edge and the biscuit slots have been cut in its ends.*

the joint, where pressure from a person sitting in the settle is concentrated. To cut the shiplaps, install a ¾" dado blade and raise it ⅜". Again, move the fence so the wood face just barely touches the blade, and then make your cuts in the top back side of each board (see Figure 3). When you've completed the shiplaps, use the same setup for rabbetting the bottom front edge of the crest rail.

For decoration, the shoulders of each tongue-and-groove board are beveled. Tilt your standard saw blade 45°, and shift the fence to the outboard side of the tilted blade. Keeping in mind that you'll have to adjust the fence for the various board widths, trim a ⅛" bevel on each edge with the blade set low so it won't cut into the tongues.

Back to the Side Panels

When the glue in the sides, seat, and bottom has dried, remove the clamps, plane the panels flat, and then cut them to length and width. Now, turn to routing the joints in the sides. Lay out the dado, groove, and rabbet locations, as shown in the side view drawing on page 11, and then set up a ¾" straight bit in your plunge router. Make the jig shown in Figure 4 on page 12. Align the jig with each dado layout, and rout the joints ⅜" deep. Add a straightedge guide to your router, and then cut the grooves and rabbets in several passes.

The side panels must be tied to each other with strong joints, and these are in part provided by the crest rail and back rail. To add more rigidity, support rails (pieces 12) are mounted inside the chest to reinforce the seat and bottom. Rip poplar stock for these four pieces, and then crosscut all the rails to length. Biscuit joinery is ideal for securing the rails to the sides, but if you don't have a biscuit joiner, you can use dowels or screws and plugs instead. Lay out the biscuit locations in the ends of the rails and on the side panels (make them dowel or screw hole locations if you

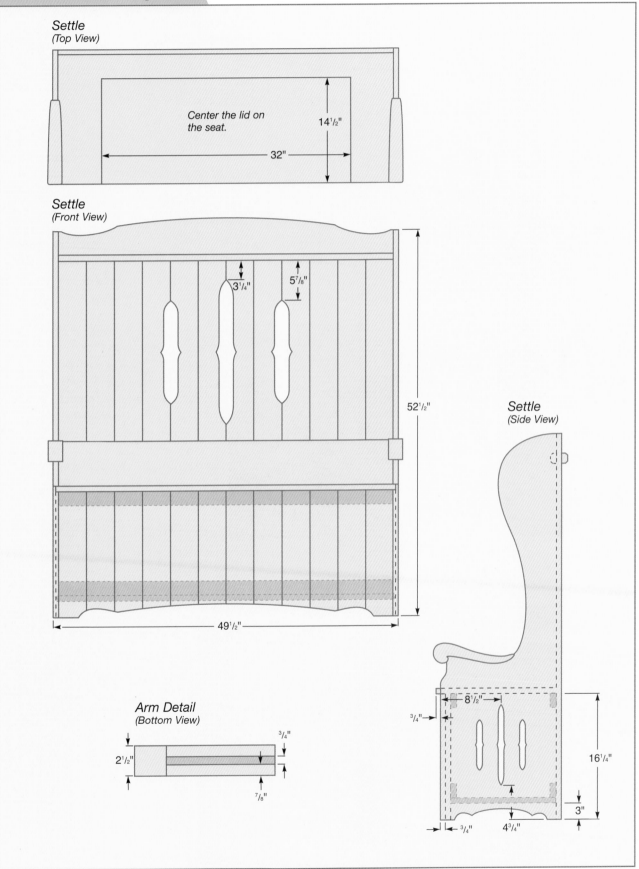

Settle
(Top View)

Center the lid on the seat.

14¹/₂"

32"

Settle
(Front View)

3¹/₄"

5⁷/₈"

52¹/₂"

Settle
(Side View)

49¹/₂"

Arm Detail
(Bottom View)

2¹/₂"

³/₄"

⁷/₈"

8¹/₂"

³/₄"

16¹/₄"

3"

³/₄"

4³/₄"

Figure 5: *Define the groove walls in the arms with a ½" slot cutter. Make one pass from each side of the arm to ensure a centered groove.*

Figure 6: *Once the walls are cut, remove the rest of the waste with a chisel, making sure to extend the groove into the crease below the knob.*

slots, and extend the grooves into the crease under each arm knob (see Figure 6).

Look at the arm side view pattern again, and you'll notice a dotted line. This line represents the finished arm shape; so retrim the pattern, and trace this new shape onto the side of each arm. Band sawing the arms to their final shape completes the tapering of the grooves. Once the arms fit the sides well, enlarge and cut out the arm's top view pattern, and trace this shape onto the stock. Band saw the sides of the arms, sand them smooth, and glue them to the settle.

Enclosing the Bench

To allow for seasonal movement, the tongue-and-groove boards should be screwed to the bench frame, but not glued. Before installing the boards, however, use a ⅜" chisel and a knife to extend the rabbet in each side panel so it matches the rabbet in the crest rail (see the rabbet detail drawing on page 13). Now, hold the left back board (piece 4) in position, and drill countersunk pilot holes into the two back support rails; then, screw the board to the frame. Work your way across the bench one board at a time, using 1⁄16"-thick shims between the boards to allow for expansion. Trim the last board to fit, if necessary, but don't secure the shiplapped ends of the boards until later.

Install the front boards (pieces 7, 8, and 9) in the same manner as the back boards, reaching into the chest to drill pilot holes and then screwing the boards to the front support rails.

Next, enlarge and cut out the patterns for the base detail of the front and back boards and for the back vent openings on page 15. Trace the base detail onto the front and back of

the bench, and cut the shapes with a jigsaw. Use the front view drawing on page 11 to position the vent openings; then, trace the patterns, and remove the waste with a jigsaw.

To cover the shiplap joint, both on the front and the back of the settle, rip a pair of trim strips (pieces 14) to width, and bevel their edges at a 30° angle. Cut one strip for the front of the settle, and clamp it in place. Secure the shiplaps and trim, drill countersunk pilot holes in the back of the crest rail, and drive in two 1¼"-long screws per board. Finish by cutting the back strip to length and tacking it in place with #4 brads.

Completing the Final Details

Because the lid must support a fair amount of weight, a continuous piano hinge (piece 15) is the best choice for securing the lid to the seat. Fortunately, this hinge is easy to install. First, cut the hinge to length, drill pilot holes, and screw it to the back edge of the lid. Then, get a friend to hold the lid in the seat opening while you secure the hinge to the seat.

Chances are, the front edge of the lid won't be even with the seat due to the combined thickness of the hinge leaves, so you'll need to plane it flush. While you're working on the seat edge, use a file to round the corners into the side panels.

With some edge filing, the bench is ready for a finish. You can use almost any stain type or color you want on your bench, but be sure to sample the stain on scrap pieces before applying it to the whole project. You may want to use a washcoat of stain controller first to prevent blotching. The stain I used on this bench was Minwax dark walnut. This gave the pine a ruddy brown color, creating an antique appearance. Following the stain, apply two coats of a tung oil finish before putting this handsome settle to use.

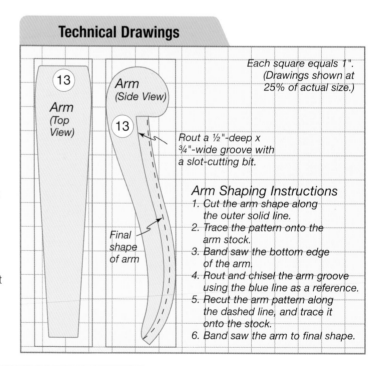

Technical Drawings

13

Arm (Top View)

Arm (Side View)

13

13

Final shape of arm

Each square equals 1". (Drawings shown at 25% of actual size.)

Rout a ½"-deep x ¾"-wide groove with a slot-cutting bit.

Arm Shaping Instructions

1. Cut the arm shape along the outer solid line.
2. Trace the pattern onto the arm stock.
3. Band saw the bottom edge of the arm.
4. Rout and chisel the arm groove using the blue line as a reference.
5. Recut the arm pattern along the dashed line, and trace it onto the stock.
6. Band saw the arm to final shape.

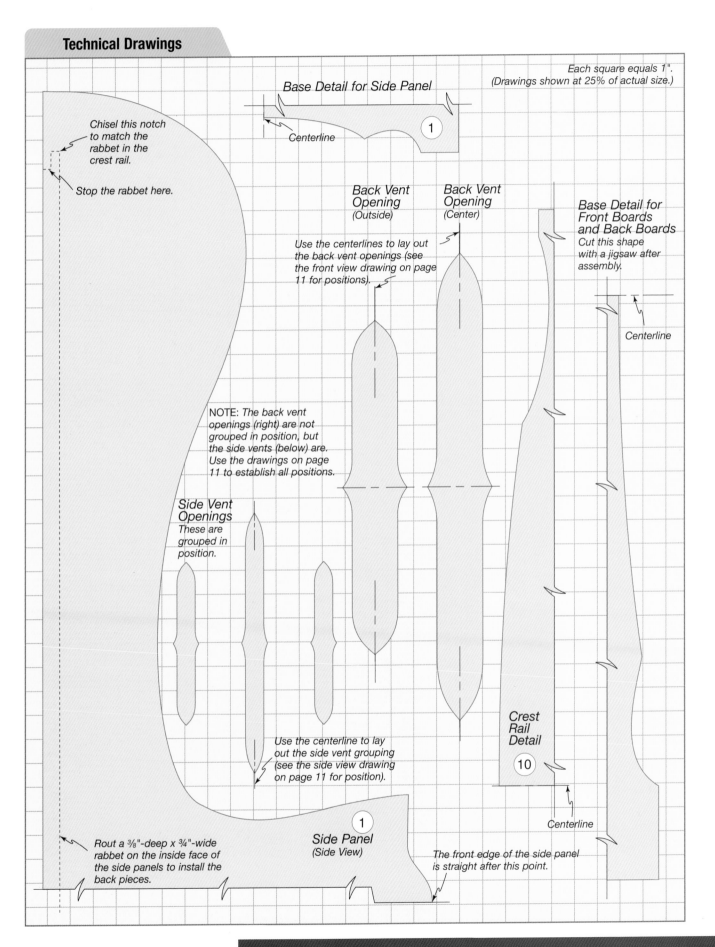

Each square equals 1".
(Drawings shown at 25% of actual size.)

Base Detail for Side Panel

1

Centerline

Chisel this notch to match the rabbet in the crest rail.

Stop the rabbet here.

Back Vent Opening
(Outside)

Back Vent Opening
(Center)

Use the centerlines to lay out the back vent openings (see the front view drawing on page 11 for positions).

Base Detail for Front Boards and Back Boards
Cut this shape with a jigsaw after assembly.

Centerline

NOTE: The back vent openings (right) are not grouped in position, but the side vents (below) are. Use the drawings on page 11 to establish all positions.

Side Vent Openings
These are grouped in position.

Use the centerline to lay out the side vent grouping (see the side view drawing on page 11 for position).

Crest Rail Detail

10

Centerline

1

Side Panel
(Side View)

The front edge of the side panel is straight after this point.

Rout a 3/8"-deep x 3/4"-wide rabbet on the inside face of the side panels to install the back pieces.

by Jim Jacobson

Frame-and-Panel Entry Bench

Every home's entryway could use a handy little bench like this. It serves double duty as a sturdy seat and a convenient storage chest. And with its raised panels and compact size, it makes an attractive addition to any foyer, large or small.

On sloppy winter days, wouldn't it be great to have a place in your entryway to sit down while you put on or pull off your boots? And wouldn't it be wonderful to have a handy spot near the door for stashing your hats and gloves? This sturdy little bench will fill the bill—and it's a gem of a project to work on, too. The front and sides feature raised panels, the seat doubles as a lid to the storage chest, and the top sports an attractive shadowbox-style trim.

Building the Frames First

The most logical starting point for this project is to create the raised-panel frames, as these form the skeleton of the bench. For this operation, you'll need to borrow or invest in a stile-and-rail set. That's a router bit (or a matched pair of router bits) that mills perfectly mated profiles on stiles and rails. You can find these bits in beading, ogee, chamfer, or concave profiles.

Rip stock for all the stiles and rails (pieces 1 through 8) about 1/16" larger in each dimension than the measurements given in the Material List on page 20. Joint the stock to final dimensions, and then trim the ends to length.

To Make or to Buy Raised Panels?

I'll confess to a temptation to buy raised panels for this entry bench rather than build them. Depending on where you shop, you can have your panels made by a custom cabinet shop for not much more than the cost of materials—especially when you factor in about $200 for buying the raised-panel and rail-and-stile bit sets to do it yourself. If you're just getting into woodworking, or if you don't own a router table and a midsize or larger router yet, buying the panels is wise. However, if you're wondering if making the panels and frames is worth the fuss, I'll definitely say yes! This may be because I am really a purist at heart and just plain enjoy the process of making a project from beginning to end. There's also something to be said for trying out new bits and techniques now and again. That's what keeps woodworking fresh and interesting. And using bits for building raised panels doesn't require nerves of steel. Just follow the bit manufacturer's instructions carefully and work safely.

Using the Stile-and-Rail Set

Lay out your stiles and rails on the workbench (just butt them together for now), and mark the matching pairs where they meet. I like to use *AA*, *BB*, and so on, to keep the parts oriented correctly during the milling process.

Chuck what I call a bead-and-groove cutter into your router, and set the bit height. Practice on a piece of scrap (the exact dimensions of your actual stock) until the profile matches the elevations shown in the drawings on pages 18–19. This cutter will create the bead on the edge of the stile, plus the groove for the panel (see Figure 1 on page 22). It's a good idea to make these cuts in two or three passes, to get a clean profile safely. Mill one edge of each rail and the six outer stiles, and mill both edges of the front center stile. Then, install a cope-and-tenoning cutter. This might be a separate bit or a rearrangement of your first setup; look at the manufacturer's

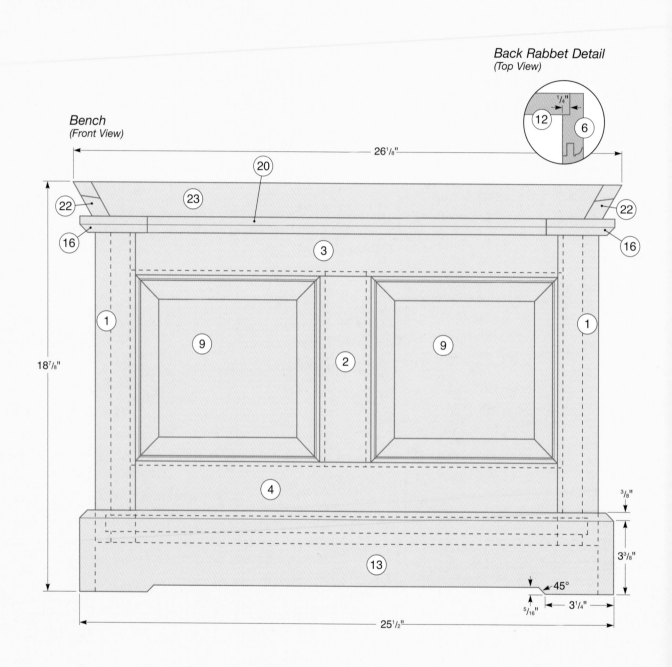

Back Rabbet Detail
(Top View)

Bench
(Front View)

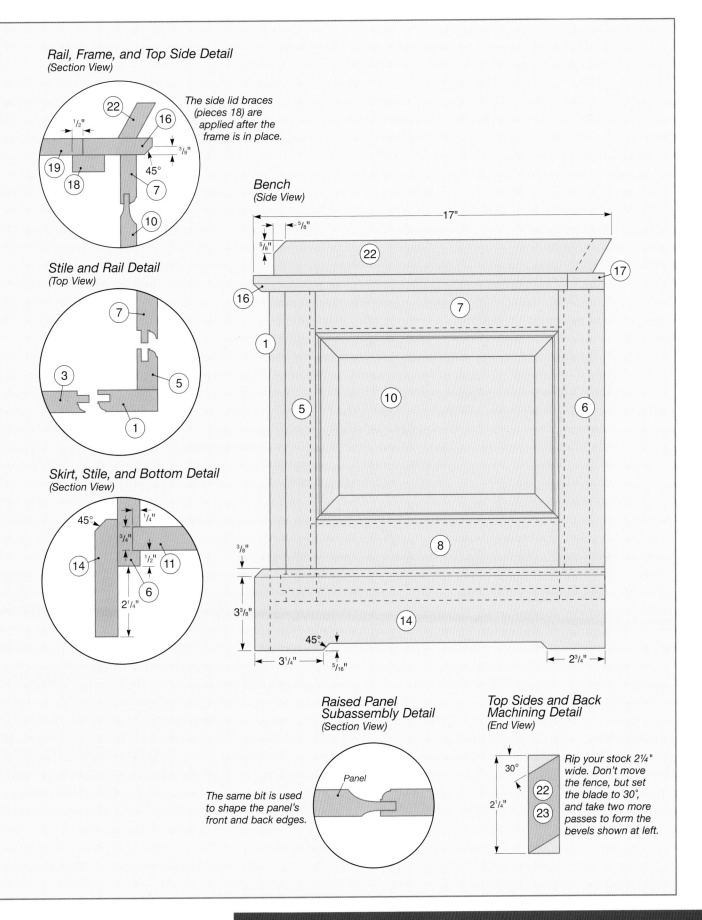

Rail, Frame, and Top Side Detail
(Section View)

22

16

1/2"

3/8"

19

18

45°

7

10

The side lid braces
(pieces 18) are
applied after the
frame is in place.

Stile and Rail Detail
(Top View)

7

3

5

1

Skirt, Stile, and Bottom Detail
(Section View)

45°

1/4"

3/4"

14

1/2"

11

6

2 1/4"

Bench
(Side View)

17"

5/8"

5/8"

22

16

17

7

1

5

10

6

8

3/8"

3 3/8"

14

45°

3 1/4"

5/16"

2 3/4"

**Raised Panel
Subassembly Detail**
(Section View)

The same bit is used
to shape the panel's
front and back edges.

Panel

**Top Sides and Back
Machining Detail**
(End View)

30°

2 1/4"

22

23

Rip your stock 2 1/4 "
wide. Don't move
the fence, but set
the blade to 30°,
and take two more
passes to form the
bevels shown at left.

Material List

		T x W x L
1	Front Outer Stiles (2)	¾" x 2³⁄₁₆" x 14¼"
2	Front Center Stile (1)	¾" x 2⁷⁄₁₆" x 8¹³⁄₁₆"
3	Front Top Rail (1)	¾" x 2³⁄₁₆" x 20⅛"
4	Front Bottom Rail (1)	¾" x 3¾" x 28½"
5	Side Front Stiles (2)	¾" x 1⁷⁄₁₆" x 14¼"
6	Side Back Stiles (2)	¾" x 2³⁄₁₆" x 14¼"
7	Side Top Rails (2)	¾" x 2³⁄₁₆" x 12⅛"
8	Side Bottom Rails (2)	¾" x 3¾" x 12⅛"
9	Front Panels (2)	¾" x 8⅞" x 8¹¹⁄₁₆"
10	Side Panels (2)	¾" x 12" x 8¹¹⁄₁₆"
11	Bottom (1)	¾" x 15⅝" x 23¼"
12	Back (1)	¾" x 13" x 23¼"
13	Front Skirt (1)	¾" x 3¾" x 25½"
14	Side Skirts (2)	¾" x 3¾" x 16¾"
15	Lid Brace, Front (1)	¾" x ½" x 22½"
16	Top Frame, Sides (2)	¾" x 3¼" x 15"
17	Top Frame, Back (1)	¾" x 1¾" x 25½"
18	Lid Brace, Sides (2)	¾" x 1½" x 14"
19	Lid (1)	¾" x 12⅞" x 18⅞"
20	Lid Cap (1)	¾" x 2" x 18⅞"
21	Piano Hinge (1)	1½" (Brass Finish)
22	Top Sides (2)	¾" x 2¼" x 16⅛"
23	Top Back (1)	¾" x 2¼" x 26⅛"

instructions for details. Use some scrap to set the height and test your fit, and then mill both ends of the front center stile and both ends of each of the rails (see Figure 2 on page 22).

Making the Panels

Glue two or three well-matched boards together for each panel (pieces 9 and 10). Be sure to select stock with color and grain that is so similar that the final joint becomes almost invisible. After cutting the panels to size, you can mill both the front and back profiles with the same router bit. I used a vertical panel-raising bit (see Figure 3 on page 22) because its cutting edges are closer to the shaft than those on traditional horizontal bits, which makes it more stable: The tip of the bit actually travels at a slower speed. You can also use a vertical bit safely in a midsize router.

Make each profile in several passes, with your router set to an appropriate speed. Machine the panels across the grain first, to minimize tearout, and clamp a high auxiliary fence to your router table fence to stabilize the workpiece.

Assembling the Frames and Panels

Sand the frame elements. Then, apply stain (if you plan on staining your bench) to the panels; this will prevent color gaps later, if the panels move after finishing. Glue and clamp the frames together, with the panels floating freely in their grooves. If you glue the panels in place, they may split as the wood reacts to changes in humidity.

Make sure the assemblies are flat and square as you apply the clamps. You can add a sandbag if needed. When the glue has set, plow dadoes for the bottom (piece 11) and rabbets for the back panel (piece 12). Their dimensions and locations are shown in the drawings on pages 18–19.

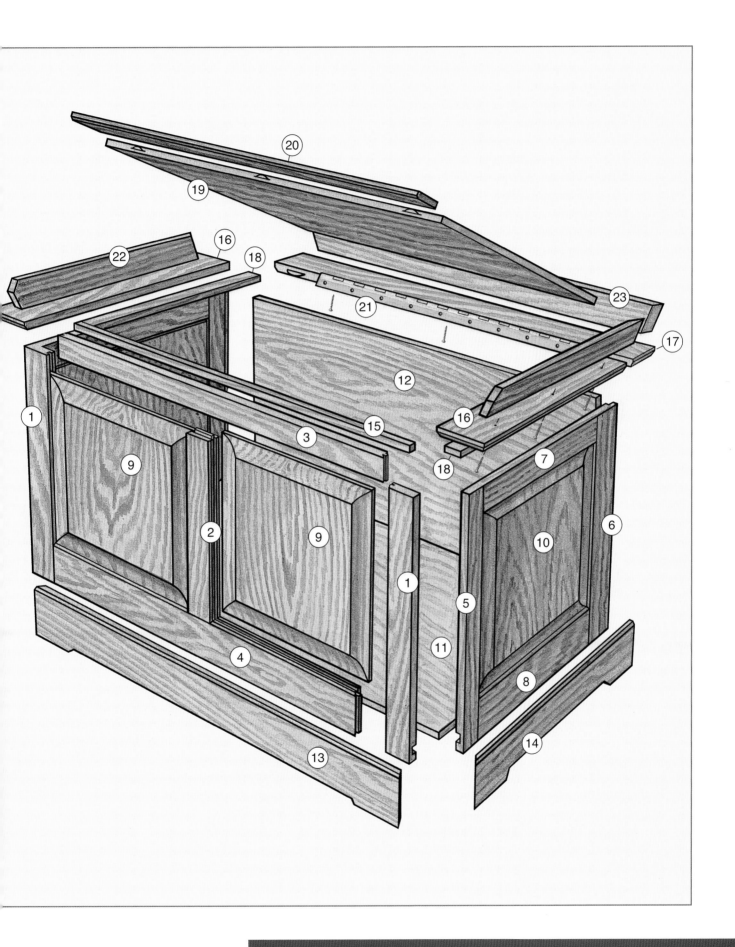

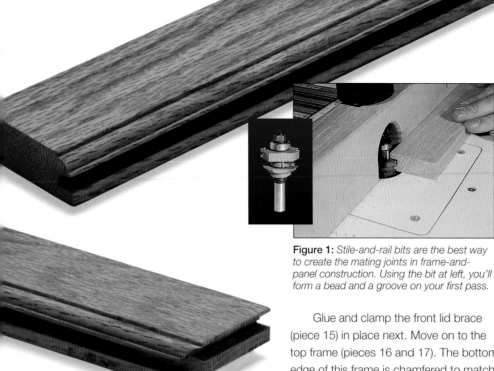

Glue and clamp the side frames to the front frame, as shown in the drawing on page 21. While a simple butt joint is quite adequate here, you may want to use biscuits to help align the parts. Slide the bottom into its dado to help keep things square. Then, predrill for a couple of 4d finish nails in each side, to hold the back in place while it's being glued and clamped. (For stability, I used oak-veneered MDF [medium-density fiberboard] for the bottom and back.) Set and fill the nail heads, and sand the filler smooth when it's dry.

Adding the Skirt and Top

When the carcass glue has dried, rip and joint a board that's long enough to yield the front and side skirts (pieces 13 and 14). Mill a chamfer on the top edge (see the drawings on pages 18–19) using a router bit. Machine the three skirts to length, and then band saw reliefs on their bottom edges, as shown in the drawings. Using your table saw's miter gauge, miter the skirts to wrap around the box. Install the skirts with glue and clamps. Temporarily clamp a plywood straightedge to the carcass to keep the skirts aligned as you clamp them in place.

Figure 1: *Stile-and-rail bits are the best way to create the mating joints in frame-and-panel construction. Using the bit at left, you'll form a bead and a groove on your first pass.*

Glue and clamp the front lid brace (piece 15) in place next. Move on to the top frame (pieces 16 and 17). The bottom edge of this frame is chamfered to match the top edge of the skirt. Chamfer the ends of the frame back, and then glue it to the carcass. With the frame back already in place, it's a little easier to locate the chamfers on the edges of the top frame sides for a perfect fit. Use biscuits on the ends of the frame sides to help glue and clamp them into place. Then, position and glue the side lid braces (pieces 18) under the frame sides.

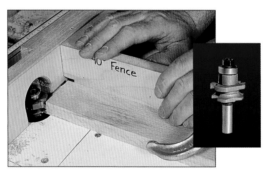

Figure 2: *Using a cope-and-tenoning cutter, machine the rail ends to fit into the grooves formed by the first cutter.*

Figure 3: *Use a raised-panel bit to raise both sides of the panels.*

Installing the Lid

The lid is a panel of veneered MDF (piece 19) with a strip of solid oak (piece 20) edge glued to it. Pick up the skirt's chamfer on the front edge of this edging, and then dry fit the seat (allow for the depth of the hinge as you do). Trim the hinge (piece 21) to length, predrill for its screws, and install it.

Follow the directions in Making Shadowbox Miter Cuts on page 23 to make the top sides and back (pieces 22 and 23). Then, glue and screw these pieces in place. Predrill for the screws, and countersink their heads.

Finishing Up

Remove the lid hinge, and sand all the parts down through the grits to 220. Apply the stain of your choice (I used a red-oak tint to even out the wood's natural colors), followed by three coats of clear finish. Reinstall the hinge, and you're finally ready to put on your boots in comfort.

Making Shadowbox Miter Cuts

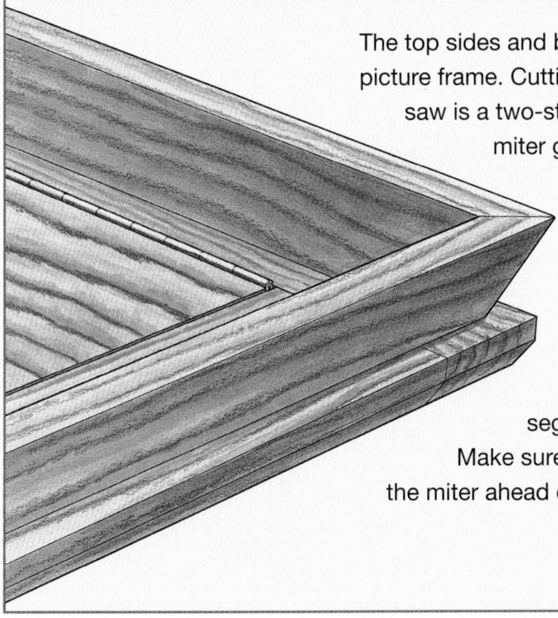

The top sides and back are milled just like a shadowbox picture frame. Cutting their compound miters on a table saw is a two-step operation. Begin by adjusting the miter gauge and blade angles using the chart at right. The Desired Incline is the angle the seat side makes with the top (in this case, 60°). Cut one end of each frame piece with the miter gauge set for a left-to-right downward slope. Then, reverse the miter gauge exactly 90°, and reposition the frame segment for the cut at the other end. Make sure the piece is oriented with the toe of the miter ahead of the heel, and then make your cuts.

Desired Incline	Blade Angle	Miter Gauge Angle
5°	43¾°	85°
10°	44¼°	80¼°
15°	43¼°	75½°
20°	41¾°	71¼°
25°	40°	67°
30°	37¾°	63½°
35°	35¼°	60¼°
40°	32½°	57¼°
45°	30°	54¾°
50°	27°	52½°
55°	24°	50¾°
60°	21°	49°

*Quick*Tip

Three-Spoke Clamp Pads

Positioning a pad between the jaw of a bar clamp and the assembly you're building can be tricky. Trying to keep the clamps in position—especially when you're at the other end of a large cabinet or panel—can be downright frustrating. These three-spoke pads solve both problems at once. Two of the three spokes become the stand's legs (they even allow for uneven surfaces), while the third spoke automatically centers itself as a hands-free pad between the metal of the clamp jaw and the workpiece being glued up. No more pads slipping out of place—and these will never get lost!

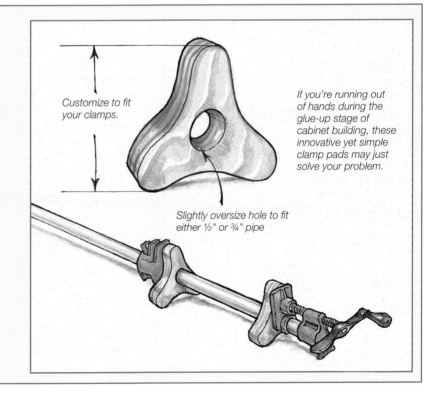

Customize to fit your clamps.

Slightly oversize hole to fit either ½" or ¾" pipe

If you're running out of hands during the glue-up stage of cabinet building, these innovative yet simple clamp pads may just solve your problem.

by John English

Portable Folding Bench for Two

Imagine this: Your team has just scored its twenty-seventh run, and it's still the bottom of the sixth. Most fans have been sitting on damp grass for a couple of hours already. No, this isn't a bad day in the majors—it's worse: You're a parent at Tuesday night Little League, and it's a doubleheader. The good news is, you're sitting on this super bench.

Actually, as every parent really knows, Little League baseball is great fun. In fact, the only true downside to a long evening of spectating is having to sit in one of those horrible chairs—you know, those flimsy nylon contraptions that fold up, usually while you're still in them! What we need is a comfortable bench that can hold two weary parents and still fit in the trunk. Well, you're in luck, because that's exactly what this project is—a lightweight, strong, weather-resistant bench that, when folded, protrudes a mere 3" from the garage wall or trunk floor.

The inspiration for this bench came from a similar design that dates from the early 1940s. It was made of weather-resistant white oak, so that's the species I chose for this project.

Building the Seat

The best way to get started on this project is to cut all the parts to the dimensions given in the Material List on page 27. Then, begin the milling process by working on the seat subassembly. The two seat supports (pieces 1) are shaped pieces; their profile is shown in the seat support drawing on page 29. Cut them to shape on your band saw, and then clean up the kerf marks with a drum sander in the drill press.

Figure 1: *The holes for the pivot hinges in the legs and seat supports are drilled in two stages, changing from a 1" bit to a ½" bit.*

Stay at the drill press to bore holes for the pivot hinges (pieces 2) and the dowel stretcher (piece 3) at the locations shown on the seat support drawing. Note that the holes for the hinges step down from 1" in diameter to ½", requiring a change of bits (see Figure 1).

Now, turn your attention to the seat slats (pieces 4). Four of the five slats are simply rounded over on their top edges with a ¼"-radius router bit and screwed in place (see the drawings on pages 26–27). Counterbore for the short screws (pieces 5) with a ⅜" Forstner bit; these will later be filled with oak plugs (pieces 6) to protect your family from sunbaked screw heads. Drive the screws home, but don't use any glue yet. You'll remove the slats during the assembly process.

Figure 2: *Various elements of the back leg assembly are rounded over with a ¼"-radius router bit. These cuts are stopped.*

The fifth and middle slat is rabbeted on each end (before rounding over the top edges) so the back legs have room to pivot (see the detail drawing on page 27). You can cut these rabbets on your table saw with a dado head, using the miter gauge to keep the cuts square to the end of the slat. Now, secure this final slat to the seat supports with the same screws.

Making the Back Leg Subassembly

This subassembly is made up of the two back legs (pieces 7), two rails (pieces 8 and 9), and a couple of diagonal braces (pieces 10). Create a radius on the top of each leg with your band saw (see the back leg drawing on page 29), and sand it smooth. Cut the 55° miter on the bottom of each leg using a table saw

with the miter gauge set at 35°. A similar setup can be used to create the 45° miters on both ends of the braces.

Drill ⅛" pilot holes through the bottom rail (see the subassembly drawing on page 26 for the locations), and then counterbore for the heads of the long screws (pieces 11). Dry fit the braces to the bottom rail, and extend the pilot holes with a ³⁄₃₂" bit. Apply Titebond II or a similar water-resistant glue to the joint, and drive the screws home.

Attach the top rail to the braces in much the same fashion, only this time use the short screws. Be careful that your pilot holes follow the drawing exactly, as there is little room for error here. Now,

Figure 3: *Installing the weather-resistant pivot hinges is a simple matter of lining up the two sides of each hinge and bolting them together.*

drill countersunk pilot holes through the legs, and glue and screw them to the rails. Make sure this subassembly is perfectly flat, and then set it aside to dry. Once the glue has dried, round over all the areas shown on the drawing using a ¼" roundover bit in your router table (see Figure 2 on page 25).

Assembling the Backrest

Referring to the drawing on page 27, cut the profile on the top edge of the backrest's top rail (piece 12), and then sand it smooth. Round over both the top and bottom edges with the same ¼" router bit you used on the seat and legs earlier, and then drill ⅛" pilot holes at the locations shown on the drawing.

Countersink these holes on the rear face of the top rail. Next, turn your attention to the two backrest stiles (pieces 13). These are also shaped pieces, and their profile is shown in the backrest stile drawing on page 29. Cut them on the band saw, round over the areas indicated (use the ¼"-radius bit), and then break all the other edges with sandpaper. Use the drawing to locate the holes for the dowel and pivot hinges, and drill them on your drill press. Be aware of the stepped nature of the pivot hinge holes, as well as which side is drilled with the larger bit (see Installing Pivot Hinges at right).

Clamp the top rail to the stiles. Then, extend the pilot holes with a ³⁄₃₂" bit, apply glue, and drive the screws in snug.

At this time, you can also round over the two lower rails (pieces 14 and 15) and drill countersunk pilot holes in them. But don't attach them to the uprights yet—you'll see why during the next step of the assembly.

Moving to the Front Legs

The front legs (pieces 16) are simply cut to shape on the band saw (see the front leg drawing on page 29) and then sanded. Miter their bottom ends on the table saw, and drill each leg in two locations for the pivot hinges (see the drawing for locations). Now, you're ready to dry assemble the whole project. The pivot hinges are the key to this assembly, so let's take a closer look at them.

Installing the Pivot Hinges

The drawing of the pivot hinge (above, right) gives you a good idea of how this inexpensive but wonderful piece of weather-resistant hardware works. One end is fixed in place by a combination of knurled teeth and a pair of screws. The other end is threaded, allowing you to secure the second (moving) piece of wood to the fixed piece with a nut (see Figure 3). A sleeve placed over the middle of the hinge ensures that you don't overtighten the nut, and it also prevents any friction buildup.

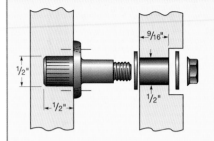
With the holes for your hinges already drilled at the proper locations, you can go ahead and secure all the knurled ends of the hinges in place. Predrill for the screws that come with the hinges to avoid splitting, and locate these screws so they aren't exactly in line with the grain of the wood.

You have already drilled four holes for the stretcher (piece 3)—one hole in each seat support and another in each of the backrest stiles. Now, chuck a sanding drum in your portable drill, and enlarge these holes slightly—enough so that the dowel passes freely through them without much play.

Slip the dowel through the holes in the seat supports, and then attach the backrest in the same manner. Secure the stretcher in the backrest uprights with retainer pins (pieces 17), glued into holes drilled through both pieces. Attach the back leg assembly (temporarily remove the screws in the seat slats to do this), and then install the spacers, nuts, and washers that come with the hinges.

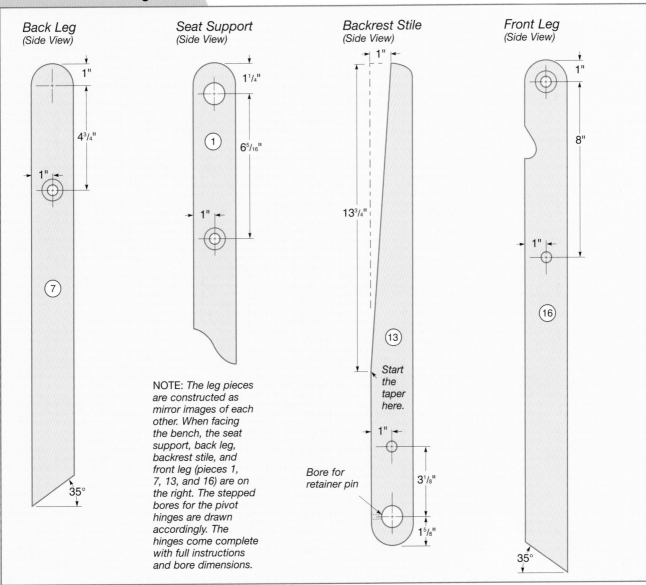

Back Leg (Side View)

1"

4³/₄"

1"

⑦

35°

Seat Support (Side View)

1¹/₄"

①

6⁵/₁₆"

1"

NOTE: *The leg pieces are constructed as mirror images of each other. When facing the bench, the seat support, back leg, backrest stile, and front leg (pieces 1, 7, 13, and 16) are on the right. The stepped bores for the pivot hinges are drawn accordingly. The hinges come complete with full instructions and bore dimensions.*

Backrest Stile (Side View)

1"

13³/₄"

⑬

Start the taper here.

Bore for retainer pin

1"

3¹/₈"

1⁵/₈"

Front Leg (Side View)

1"

8"

1"

⑯

35°

Wrapping Up Construction

Apply waterproof glue to the seat slats, and drive the screws home for the last time. Glue oak plugs into the screw counterbores. I used button plugs with domed tops to make sure the rain runs off. Measure diagonally in both directions to verify that the seat is square before the glue dries, and tweak it if it's not. Slip the front legs in place; install the spacers, washers, and nuts; and fold the bench into its closed position.

The last step in the assembly is to install the two lower rails of the backrest—the ones you held aside a while back. The idea is to ensure that the backrest rails fit neatly on either side of the front seat slat when the bench is folded. Instead of relying on the drawing, simply fold the backrest down, and position the rails on either side of the front slat. Once they're positioned, drill the pilot holes and countersinks, and then attach the rails to the stiles with the short screws.

Applying Finish

I wanted this bench to last at least as long as the original—which was built around World War II—so I sprayed it with exterior polyurethane. With all its slat nooks and narrow parts, this project really lends itself to spraying rather than brushing. If you don't own spray equipment, a couple of aerosol cans will do a respectable job. To avoid exposure to the fumes, spray the bench outdoors. After all, that's where this handy, lightweight folding bench belongs.

Hoop-Back Garden Bench

Graceful curves give this bench a timeless style, while reclaimed cypress lumber ensures that it will stand up to the worst weather, season after season. As far as outdoor projects go, this bench requires a fairly ambitious effort and several weekends to complete, but its rugged construction will be your reward.

by Chris Marshall

If your patio seating amounts to a couple of plastic chairs or a backless picnic bench, maybe it's time to add one of these garden benches to your list of options. At more than 5' long, it will easily seat three adults. The gentle angle of the backrest and the close spacing of the seat slats make it quite comfortable, as well.

The project's design could have been simplified by involving fewer curves, but a curvy bench seems to harmonize well with the irregular shapes of outdoor spaces and flower beds. The armrests and the crest rail, in particular, make the bench feel more organic, informal, and inviting.

A weather-resistant wood species is a must for this project. I used reclaimed sinker cypress (see The Lowdown on Sinker Cypress on page 32), and it was a pleasure to build with. Cypress cuts, routs, and sands similar to cedar or redwood. It's not oily, it has a pleasant scent, and it glues up without

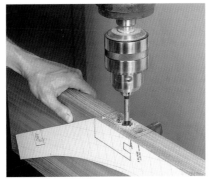

Figure 1: *Attach a leg template to each leg blank, and leave it there for the entire machining process. Drill the mortise for the seat rail before you cut the back leg out of its blank.*

issue. Take the usual precautions when cutting or routing to minimize end-grain tearout and splintering.

Templates and More Templates
Laying out and assembling this bench will go much easier if you start with some full-size patterns and templates. Make a full-size gridded pattern of the bench's end view—it'll be a real help for positioning the armrests and setting up the rail angles. You should also fabricate hardboard templates for the crest rail, back leg, armrest (both side and top views), seat rail, and front rail. These templates will be handy for locating

mortises and for template routing the rough parts to final shape. Use the elevation drawings printed throughout this article to make these shop aids. It's worth the fuss.

Making the End Frames
Get rolling on this project by building the end frames, which consist of the back and front legs and the seat and lower rails (pieces 1 through 4). Refer to the Material List on page 34 for dimensions.

Start with the back legs. Use your back leg template to draw the leg shapes on some 8½"-wide stock. Orient the leg shapes so the longest flat edges of the legs line up with a stock edge. I suggest that you stick the template to each leg blank with hot-melt glue or double-sided tape. Mark the seat rail mortises, and cut them using whatever machining method you prefer (see Figure 1). (I drilled them out with a Forstner bit.) Then, cut out the leg shapes, and refine them with a piloted,

The Lowdown on Sinker Cypress

During the late 1800s and early 1900s, loggers used rivers for transporting logs to lumber mills. In southern states, much of this timber was virgin cypress, ranging in age from 300 to 1,200 years old. Some logs sank while in transit, where they've remained largely preserved under layers of

Recovered "sinker" cypress logs remained largely preserved under layers of oxygen-poor mud and silt for over a century.

mud and silt. Krantz Recovered Woods, my lumber supplier for this bench, harvests these "sinker" logs from Louisiana lakes and rivers. The logs are sawn into boards and beams and then thoroughly air-dried before they're sold.

Virgin cypress trees matured slowly in dense, ancient forests. Recovered logs exhibit a whopping 30 to 50 annual growth rings per inch! The trees in today's second-growth forests average only 5 to 10 rings per inch. Higher ring counts make antique cypress exceptionally stable,

fine grained, largely free of knots, and naturally resistant to insects and rot.

Krantz offers sinker cypress in 4/4, 8/4, and beam thicknesses, in widths up to 12" and in lengths up to 30'. To learn more or to receive a price quote on lumber, call Krantz Recovered Woods at 888-242-1050, or visit them on the Web at *www.krantzrecoveredwoods.com*.

Figure 2: *To rout the angled shoulders on the back legs' top tenons (right), make a jig that registers the angles, and clamp it to both legs (above). That way, you can mill them in one setup. A rub collar on your router can follow the angled jig shapes to cut the shoulders. Flip the legs over in the jig to make the second set of angled shoulders.*

flush-trimming bit in the router table; this will save loads of sanding time. Cut the lower rail mortises with a router, a ¾" straight bit, and an edge guide. Both rail mortises are offset on the legs to create ¼" shadow lines between these parts.

Now, turn to the top leg tenons. Notice in the drawings and in the inset photo in Figure 2 that the front and back shoulders are angled to accommodate the curved crest rail. The bent leg shape won't allow for cutting these angled shoulders on a saw, but you can rout them with a simple jig, a rub collar, and a straight bit (see Figure 2, top photo). The other pair of square shoulders and cheeks on these tenons can be trimmed to shape with a band saw.

Both the seat rails and lower rails have angled tenons where they attach

to the back legs. Cut the rails to size now (but don't cut the seat rail arches yet), and make the angled shoulders of these tenons on the table saw with a wide dado and the miter gauge set to 75°. Cut the short cheeks and shoulders on the band saw. Make the straight front tenons on these parts in the usual way, and then cut the seat rail arches. Flush trim the arches at the router table, using the seat rail template as the bearing guide.

The front legs have tenons on top with angled shoulders similar to the back legs. Since these legs are straight, cut the angled shoulders at the table saw with the miter gauge set to 75°. Trim the front and back shoulders and cheeks to shape at the band saw.

Wrap up the front leg joinery by cutting mortises for the seat rails, lower rails, and front rail. Keep the orientation of the front legs clear as you mill these mortises—the legs are mirror images and not identical.

Dry fit the end frames, and then give the parts a good sanding. After that, ease the edges, and glue up the frames.

Making the Seat

Follow the Material List to cut the front and back rails and the seat supports (pieces 5 through 7) to size. Mill tenons on the ends of the front rail. Attach the front rail template temporarily, trim the broad arch in the rail about $\frac{1}{16}$" proud of the template edge, and then refine the shape with a flush-trimming bit and your router.

The back slats fit into a series of individual mortises in the back rail. Use the drawings on page 39 to lay out these mortises, and mill them (see Figure 3). Some bench designs will substitute a long, continuous mortise here and separate the slats with spacer blocks, but I wanted to minimize exposed horizontal glue lines wherever possible. The fewer joints where water can soak in and cause trouble, the better.

Figure 3: *The back slats fit into individual mortises in the back rail. A hollow chisel mortiser is the perfect tool for this repetitive chopping task. Or you could cut the mortises with a plunge router fitted with an edge guide.*

QuickTip

Storyboards Keep Part Ordering Clear
Large assemblies with numerous parts can quickly get out of hand—so the pros know the value of a storyboard in keeping everything organized. This can be as simple as a large sheet of paper or hardboard laid on the workbench, with a full-size template drawn on it. The template shows how the parts will be oriented to each other after assembly, and a good template can even be used to take measurements while you cut parts to size. Hot glue small guide blocks to the template to help line up the larger parts.

Figure 4: *To hide the seat slat fasteners, drive them in from underneath. I used a pocket hole jig and weather-resistant pocket screws. Tack the slats in place first with glue.*

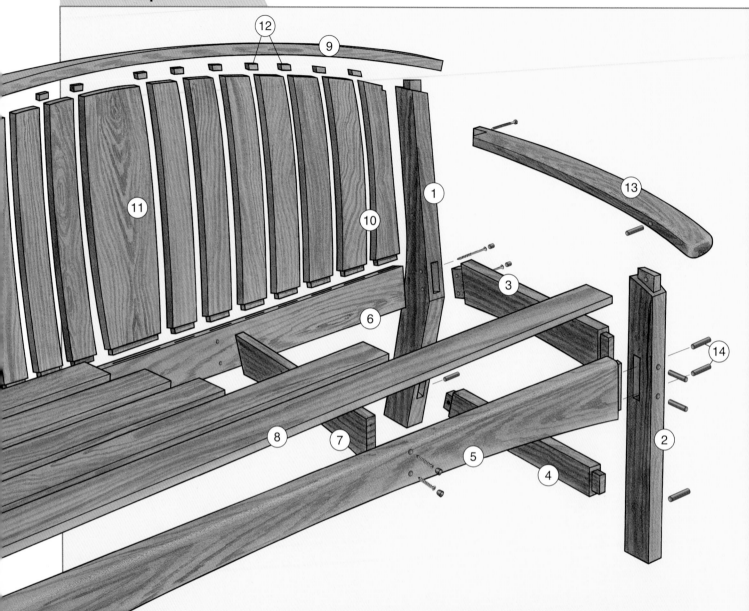

Material List

		T x W x L			T x W x L
1	Back Legs* (2)	1¾" x 8½" x 33"	**8**	Seat Slats (5)	¾" x 2¾" x 66"
2	Front Legs (2)	1¾" x 2¼" x 24¼"	**9**	Crest Rail* (1)	1¾" x 8¼" x 71¼"
3	Seat Rails (2)	1½" x 4" x 17¾"	**10**	Narrow Back Slats* (14)	¾" x 4" x Varies
4	Lower Rails (2)	1½" x 2" x 19½"	**11**	Wide Back Slat (1)	¾" x 7" x 21"
5	Front Rail (1)	1½" x 5¾" x 65"	**12**	Back Slat Spacers (14)	¾" x ¾" x 1"
6	Back Rail (1)	1½" x 4" x 62½"	**13**	Armrests (2)	4"* x 4½" x 25"
7	Seat Supports (2)	1½" x 2¾" x 16¼"	**14**	Dowel Pins (30)	⅜" Dia.

Width dimensions are prior to shaping.

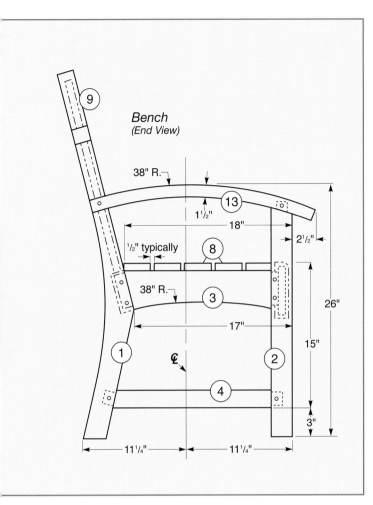

Bench
(End View)

38" R.

1¹/₂"

18"

2¹/₂"

¹/₂" typically

38" R.

17"

26"

15"

3"

11¹/₄"

11¹/₄"

Figure 5: *Rout the shallow step of the crest rail's continuous slat mortise first. Plow it from one back leg mortise to the other. Then, mill the ¾"-deep stopped portion of the slat mortise with the same bit and edge guide setup.*

The back ends of the seat supports are angled to hold the back rail in the same plane as the crest rail. That way, the back slats will fit into straight, rather than angled, mortises. Attach the seat supports to both long rails with pairs of countersunk 4" deck screws at each joint. The top edges of the seat supports should be flush with the back rail's mortised edge, but be careful that the supports attach ¾" down from the top edge of the front rail. That way, the seat slats will align with the top edge of the front rail.

Now, join the front and back rails to the end frames to erect the bench seat. The back legs attach to the back rail with pairs of countersunk 4" screws. Glue the front rail tenons into their mortises. Line up this center

bench subassembly so the back rail and seat rails align properly, as shown in the drawings.

Cut the five seat slats (pieces 8) to size, and round over the edges and ends. Instead of attaching these slats by driving screws down into the rails and seat supports, use dabs of water-resistant glue to tack them in place, and then drive weather-resistant 1½" pocket screws up from underneath (see Figure 4 on page 33). This is a good way to avoid rows of unsightly wood plugs on the seat slats.

Moving On to the Back
The curved crest rail (piece 9) is easier to machine while it's still part of a wider, flat-edged blank. Stick the template to your stock so the bottom curve faces

up and the pointed tips are flush with the stock edge. Cut the crest rail's inner curve, and trim it flush with a router. The back slats fit into a continuous groove in this curve. Refer to the drawings on page 39 to see how this mortise steps from a depth of ⁵/₁₆" to ¾" for most of the length. The shallower part of the mortise helps keep the back leg mortises strong while still hiding the top ends of the endmost back slats. Set up your router and edge guide to cut the ⁵/₁₆" mortise depth first, and mark the back leg mortise locations. Rout the shallow portion of the step from one leg mortise to the other (see Figure 5), and then continue to hog out the deeper slat mortises to a depth of ¾", stopping 1¾" from each of the back leg mortises.

Figure 6: *Drawing parallel curves on the back slats is easy if you group the slats together in a jig. Make a template with a curve based on a 9' radius, and trace the curves onto the slats using the template. Shape the slat jig so the top edge matches the crest rail mortise curve. That way, you can scribe the slat top curves, as well.*

Prototyping

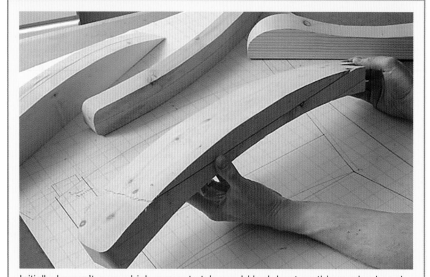

Initially, I wasn't sure which armrest style would look best on this garden bench, so I made several prototype armrests from scrap. Prototyping is a great way to help you settle form, function, and ergonomic issues, especially on a chair or bench project.

With the continuous mortise completed, bore the back leg mortises on the drill press with a 1¼"-diameter Forstner bit, and chisel the corners square. The flat bottom edge of the crest rail blank will ensure that these two mortises are square to the back legs. Once the leg mortises are done, finish cutting out the crest rail, rout it flush to the template, and ease the edges with a ¼" roundover bit.

The back slats start out as 4" or 7" straight-edged blanks but end up curved along both long edges. I tackled the task of marking these curves by butting the narrow and wide back slats (pieces 10 and 11) next to one another inside a jig (see the back slat jig on page 41). First, cut the bottom tenons on the slats, and then set them in the jig, which has a curved top that matches the shape and position of the crest rail

Figure 7: *Sawing the armrests to shape is a two-stage technique. Cut the side profile first, tape the offcuts back in place, and then cut the top profile.*

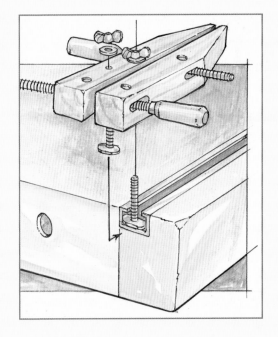

Figure 8: *Cut out a portion of your full-size bench end view pattern to make an alignment jig for drilling the front leg mortises in the armrests. The goal here is to cut these mortises so the legs meet the armrests squarely, despite the curve.*

mortise at full depth. Then, using the jig, mark the curved top line (which also determines the slat length). When you're done, flip the slats over, and rearrange them in the jig so the curved cutoff line shows on top. Use a short template in the jig to draw the curved edges on the slats, one after the next. All these curves match those on the center slat (see Figure 6). Index the curves on the slats so the finished slats will be 1" apart. Make the center slat 6" wide and the other slats 3" wide. Leave the endmost slats flat on their outer edges, where they'll meet the back legs.

Gang cut the narrow slats in stacks of three or four on the band saw, and then cut them to length individually. Smooth the slat edges. Note in the bench back drawing on page 39 that

QuickTip

Instant Workbench Vise

Most workbenches have two vises that allow you to work at either one side or an end. If your bench only has one vise at the end, here's a way to add a side vise wherever you need it. Rout a slot along your bench, and embed a length of metal T-track to hold a couple of 10" hand-screw clamps. Then, drill a hole in each clamp, and insert a T-bolt that fits in the track. A wing nut makes adjusting easy. Sliding one clamp in from each end gives you an instant workbench vise.

the endmost slats need to be notched at the top corners to fit into the crest rail mortise where it changes depth.

Test fit the slats and the crest rail on the bench. When it all assembles without force, slip the slats into the back rail and crest rail mortises dry, but glue the crest rail onto the back leg tenons. Then, cut slat spacers (pieces 12) to size, and use dabs of glue and galvanized finish nails to pin them into place in the long mortise.

Adding the Armrests
Make blanks for the armrests (pieces 13) by building up two thicknesses of 8/4 stock. Notice that the final armrest shape is curved both lengthwise and widthwise. Here's how to sculpt the shape: Use your armrest side view template to draw this portion of the curvature, and then band saw the shape. Save the offcuts, and tape them back in place to re-form the blanks. Now, use your top view armrest template to mark this dimension of the curvature onto the blank. Saw the armrest to shape (see Figure 7 on page 37), and remove all the offcuts.

If you made a full-size end view pattern of the bench, locating and making the armrest mortises for the front leg tenons will be a snap. Remove a portion of your pattern directly above the armrest, and use it as the reference for making a drilling jig that holds the armrest square, relative to the front leg. Mount this section of your pattern to some thick scrap, cut the scrap to match your pattern curvature, and attach it to a scrap base. Now,

boring the armrest mortises on the drill press will be a simple matter of clamping them against the jig, marking the mortise dimensions off the pattern, and drilling the stopped mortise holes (see Figure 8 on page 37). Square up the mortises with a sharp chisel, and refine the armrest with a good dose of belt sanding. Ease the edges with a ¼"- or ⅜"-diameter roundover bit.

Set the armrests against the front and back legs to determine where to notch the armrests so they fit around the back legs. Cut these notches out with a handsaw. Install the armrests with glue in the mortise-and-tenon joint and with a ¼" x 2" countersunk galvanized lag bolt and washer to the back legs.

Pinning the Joints
Glue alone will certainly hold these mortise-and-tenon joints for a long while, but eventually, the glue may fail. As added insurance, it's a good idea to peg all the interlocking joints and plug the screw holes with ⅜"-diameter cypress dowel pins (pieces 14). You can't buy cypress dowels, but they're easy to make on the router table with a bullnose bit. Two passes through a scrap tunnel jig turns square strips into perfect dowels (see Cypress Dowels, below, for details).

Trim the dowel pins, and sand them flush. Then, give the bench a coat of penetrating wood finish to help preserve its color. All that's left to do now is to move your new bench outside, rustle up the tiki torches, and start planning your next patio party.

Cypress Dowels

Where can you find cypress dowels? In your scrap bin. Make your dowel pegs at the router table with a ⅜"-diameter bullnose bit. Clamp a scrap tunnel against the fence to keep the dowels from chattering during milling. Run strips of square stock through the tunnel twice to round half of the curvature with each pass.

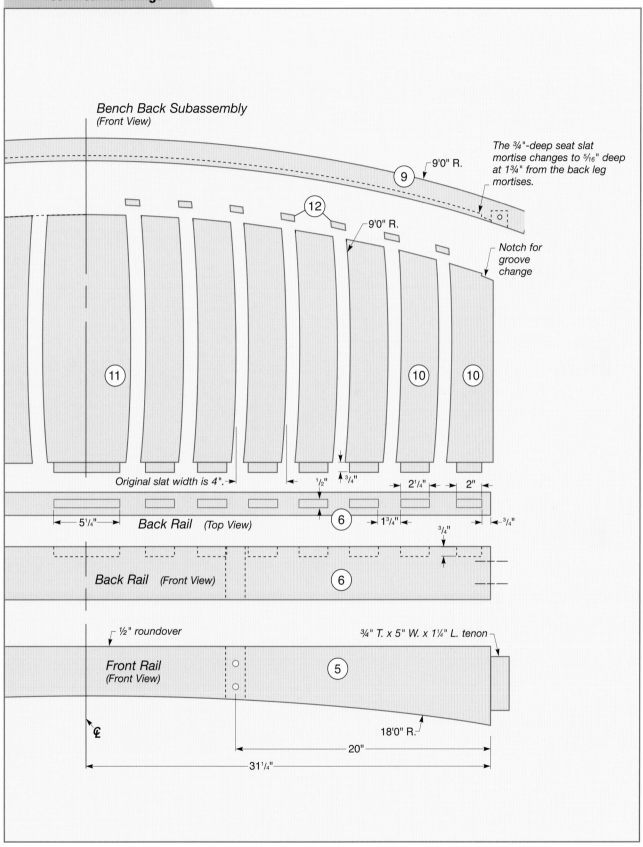

Bench Back Subassembly
(Front View)

The ¾"-deep seat slat mortise changes to ⁵⁄₁₆" deep at 1¾" from the back leg mortises.

9'0" R.

⑨

⑫

9'0" R.

Notch for groove change

⑪

⑩ ⑩

Original slat width is 4". ← ½" ¾" 2¼" 2"

5¼" **Back Rail** (Top View) ⑥ 1¾" ¾"

¾"

Back Rail (Front View) ⑥

½" roundover

¾" T. x 5" W. x 1¼" L. tenon

Front Rail
(Front View) ⑤

18'0" R.

℄

20"

31¼"

Seat Slats and Rail
(Side View)

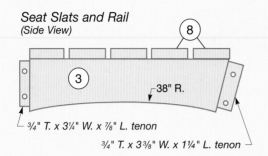

⑧

③

38" R.

¾" T. x 3¼" W. x ⅞" L. tenon

¾" T. x 3⅜" W. x 1¼" L. tenon

NOTE: *Given the shape of the back legs, you'll need to cut the upper mortises without the aid of a table saw. Use a router, a rub collar, and a jig to make these "template-style" (see page 32). The angled mortises on the front legs can be cut conventionally, since the legs are flat.*

1¼" T. x 1¼" W. x 1⅝" L. tenon at longest shoulder

17° tenon shoulder

Seat Support (Side View)

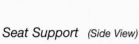

⑦

38" R.

①

31¼"

1¼" T. x 1¾" W. x 1¼" L. tenon at longest shoulder

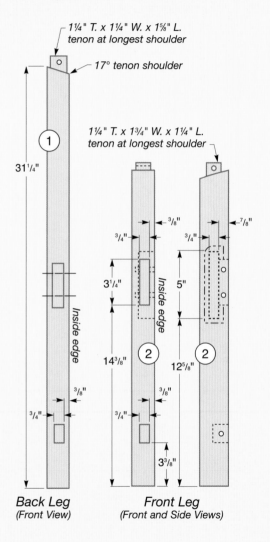

Inside edge

Inside edge

¾"

⅜"

3¼"

14⅜"

5"

¾"

⅞"

Lower Rail (Side View)

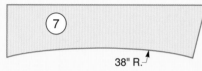

④

¾" T. x 1¼" W. x 1¼" L. tenon

¾" T. x 1½" W. x 1¼" L. tenon

②

②

⅜"

¾"

⅜"

¾"

3⅜"

12⅝"

Back Leg
(Front View)

Front Leg
(Front and Side Views)

**Back Slat
Layout Detail**

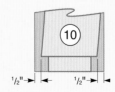

⑩

½"

½"

Although the back slats have curved edges, keep the bottom tenons straight. That way, they'll fit into straight mortises milled in the back rail.

Armrest *(Top and Side Views)*

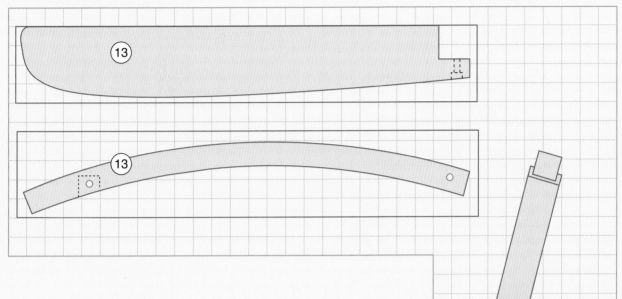

Back Slat Jig

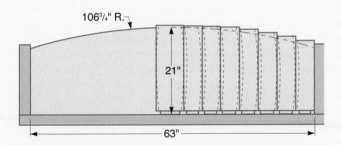

$106^{3}/_{4}$" R.

21"

63"

The key to accurately forming the back slats is to create the jig shown above. The jig's curved edge is shaped to match the crest rail mortise groove. Lay the slats in the jig, and mark their curved top ends using the curved edge of the jig. Next, flip the slats over, and move them end-for-end on the jig so the curved line you drew is showing. Then, use a template to lay out the curved edges of the slats (see Figure 6 on page 36), which are represented by the dotted lines above. There must be a 1" space between the curved parallel lines.

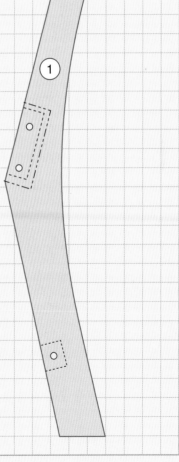

Back Leg *(Side View)*

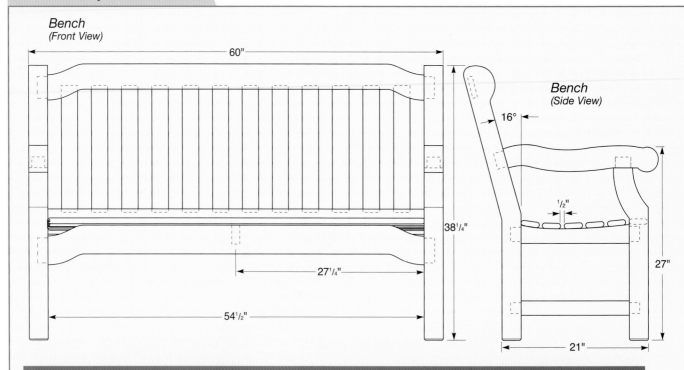

Bench
(Front View)

Bench
(Side View)

Material List

	T x W x L			T x W x L
1 Front Legs (2)	2¾" x 5¼" x 25½"		**9** Stretchers (2)	1⅜" x 2" x 18½"
2 Back Legs (2)	2¾" x 7" x 39"		**10** Back Slats (12)	½" x 2⅜" x 19"
3 Arms (2)	2¾" x 4" x 24"		**11** Seat Slats (5)	¾" x 2⅝" x 60"
4 Front Rail (1)	1⅜" x 5½" x 57½"		**12** Front Seat Slat (1)	¾" x 2⅝" x 54½"
5 Back Rail (1)	1⅜" x 3⅜" x 57½"		**13** Screws (21)	#8-2" (Exterior)
6 Crest Rail (1)	1⅜" x 4½" x 57½"		**14** Screws (18)	#8-1¼" (Exterior)
7 Side Rails (2)	1⅜" x 2⅝" x 18½"		**15** Plugs (39)	⅜" Dia. (End Grain)
8 Middle Rail (1)	1⅜" x 3" x 19"		**16** Lag Screw and Washer (1)	¼" x 2½"

shape (see Figure 1 on page 43). Cut just outside the lines, and then use a plane to smooth the flat areas that are accessible. Next, clamp the like pieces into pairs, aligning the smoothed surfaces. Then, use a belt sander, drum sander, disc sander, and rasp to work the remaining areas flush and smooth, all the while keeping an eye on the thickness of the stock, which should end up at 2¾".

Now, lay out the mortises on the legs, as shown on the patterns. All of the leg mortises are ¾" wide and 1½"

deep. To cut the mortises, first bore out the bulk of the waste with your drill press and a ¾" brad-point bit, and then clean up the sides and ends with a chisel. For the most part, drilling the mortises is straightforward, but for the mortises on the front face of each rear leg, you must prop each end of the leg up so that they're square to the bit.

The first step in cutting the tenon on the top of each front leg is done at the table saw with a ½" dado blade. Install the blade and raise it 1". Clamp a clearance block to your fence, and set

the fence to cut 1½"-long tenon cheeks. To accommodate the curved top of the leg, make a fence like the one shown in Figure 2, and screw it to your miter gauge. Cut cheeks on the sides of each leg, and then use a handsaw to cut shoulders and cheeks on the front and back of each leg.

Forming Tenons on the Rails
Next, cut your stock for the rails and stretchers to the overall sizes given in the Material List. As mentioned earlier, the widths given for a few of these

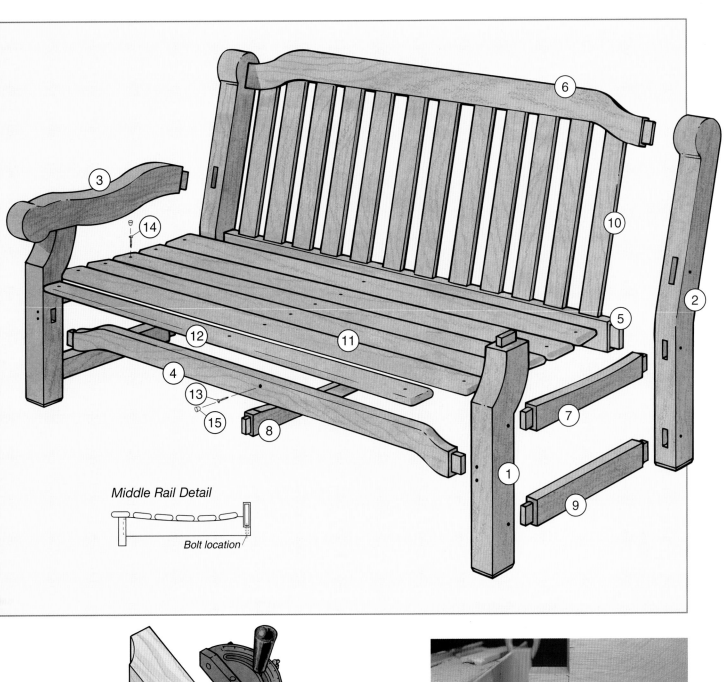

Middle Rail Detail

Bolt location

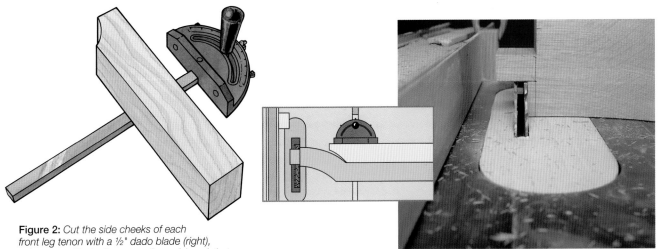

Figure 2: *Cut the side cheeks of each front leg tenon with a ½" dado blade (right), using a modified miter gauge fence (above) that fits the curve at the top of the leg (center).*

pieces are a little large to allow for shaping their curves later. However, the lengths given for all the pieces are exact; therefore, make sure you crosscut the ends squarely and accurately.

Normally, cutting tenons on the table saw would be the most efficient method, but the long bench rails are too unwieldy for this operation. In this case, using a router and an edge guide makes the most sense since you'll be moving a relatively light tool while keeping the heavy, long timber stationary.

Chuck a ¾" straight bit in your router, and attach the edge guide to the router's base. Set the depth of cut at 5⁄16", and adjust the guide for cutting 1½"-long tenons (see Figure 3). Make several passes to rout the cheeks for all the tenons on the rails and stretchers (note that the middle rail has a tenon at its front end only). Once you've finished routing the cheeks, cut ¼"-deep edge shoulders by hand on the lower back rail, the side and middle rails, and the stretchers. Hold back from making shoulder cuts on the other pieces until after they've been band sawn to shape.

Because the side rail tenons will partially butt into the tenons of the back and front rails when they all join with the legs, you will need to cut a notch in each tenon at a 45° angle. Mark these areas, and lay out the 45° angles. Then, remove the waste with a handsaw.

Next, joint one edge of each arm lamination, and rip the two pieces to the width indicated in the Material List. Now, tilt your miter gauge 16°, and crosscut the back end of each arm to match the slope of the back legs. Using a ¾" straight bit in the router, rout the arms' rear tenon cheeks to a depth of 1", and then cut the ¼"-deep edge shoulders by hand.

Figure 3: *To form the rail tenons, first cut the rail ends squarely to length, and then use a router equipped with a ¾" straight bit and a straightedge guide to cut the cheeks.*

Figure 4: *The key to getting the tightest joint possible between each arm and front leg is to plane the arm pad area as flat as you can.*

Shaping the Arms and Rails

Return to the drawings on page 49. Enlarge and cut out the patterns for the arm, crest rail, front rail, side rail, and middle rail, and trace the patterns onto your stock. Band saw the pieces to shape, and then use a handsaw to cut ¼"-deep tenon shoulders on all the pieces. Save the small triangular cutouts from the top edge of the crest

rail for use later. Now, sand all the rough band-sawn surfaces smooth, except for the flat joint pad area on the bottom of each arm.

The key to creating a tight joint between the arms and front legs is to get the joint pad on each arm as flat as possible. Most of the work can be done with a sharp block plane and a chisel, although a shoulder plane will also prove helpful. Use the block plane to work from the edges of the arms toward the center (see Figure 4), checking your work often with a square.

Once the arm pads are flat and square, mock up each leg, side rail, and stretcher assembly, and hold the arms in place to mark the front leg tenon positions. Transfer the tenon marks onto the pad area of each arm, and lay out the ¾"-wide x 1½"-deep mortises. Drill out the mortises, clean them up with a chisel, and dry fit the arms on the leg assemblies. Most likely, you'll have to tweak the fit, including the fit of the pad on the leg shoulder. When the fit of all the parts looks good, glue and clamp the pieces together to form two end assemblies.

After the glue has set for a few hours, remove the clamps, and drill counterbored pilot holes for #8-2" exterior-grade screws (pieces 13) at each joint location. The holes should be drilled into the legs and arms so that they're centered on each tenon's width and set back 5⁄8" from the joint shoulders; note that each front-rail-to-front-leg joint gets two holes, as shown in Figure 5. Pinning the joints in this way guarantees that they will never come apart. Fill the counterbores with 3⁄8" white-oak plugs (pieces 15) cut from a dowel rod.

Making the Back Frame

You've already cut the stock for the rails, formed their tenons, and band sawn the appropriate pieces to shape. Now, it's time to lay out the slat mortises on the crest rail and back rail (see the slat mortise detail drawing on page 48).

Although it's tedious work, the best way to rough in the slat mortises is with a drill press and a ⁷⁄₁₆" brad-point bit (use this smaller bit, and then chisel the mortises to their full ½" width). Or use a mortising machine with a ½" hollow-point chisel.

Begin working on the crest rail by taping the triangular cutouts back into place on its top edge to help keep the piece steady throughout the drilling operation. Now, clamp a fence to your drill press table so it aligns the bit with the center of the rail stock. Adjust the drill press table height to allow the entire rail to pass below the bit, and set the depth stop for ⁹⁄₁₆"-deep holes (the mortises in the curves at the ends of the piece will be deeper at this setting). Bore the holes, first drilling at the ends of each mortise layout and then working across the remaining area. If you used a drill press for this work, square the mortise ends and clean up the walls with chisels.

To drill mortises in the back rail, start by making a jig for holding the stock at a 16° angle to the bit (see Figure 6 on page 48). Once the jig has been made, clamp it to the drill press table so the stock is squarely centered under the bit, adjust the depth stop for ⁹⁄₁₆"-deep holes, and drill the holes just as you did in the crest rail.

Clamp the two rails against each other to compare the slat mortise positions, and refine them if necessary. Cut all the back slats (pieces 10) to size,

and test their fit in your rail mortises. Once you're confident in the fit of the slats, chamfer their ends a little with a belt sander to ease the final assembly and provide a relief area for glue.

The tenon on the front end of the middle rail fits into a mortise on the inside of the front rail (see the drawings on pages 44–45). Lay out the mortise, making sure it is located ¼" down from the top edge of the rail, and then rough it in with a drill bit. Use a chisel for cleanup.

The next stage of the bench assembly is awkward, and an extra set of hands will help. First, put a little glue in each slat mortise, and then draw the back frame together with bar clamps. Next, spread glue in the leg mortises of one end assembly and on the corresponding tenons of the back frame and front rail. Slip these assemblies together, and then repeat the gluing steps for the other end. Use long bar clamps to pull everything together tightly for a few hours.

Position the middle rail in the bench to mark the notch at its back end where it meets the back rail (see the middle rail detail drawing on page 45). Now, cut the 1½"-deep notch, and test the fit of the piece in the bench. If the fit is right, remove the middle rail to drill the counterbored through hole for the lag screw and washer (piece 16). Now, replace the piece in the bench, and continue the pilot hole into the back rail. Again, pull out the piece to put glue in the mortise and on the notch. Then, install the piece, and drive in the lag screw. Finish up by cross-pinning all the new joints in the bench.

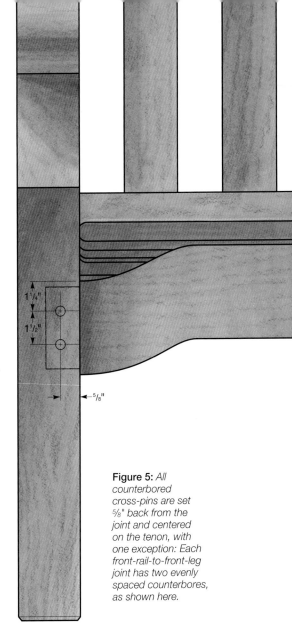

Figure 5: *All counterbored cross-pins are set ⅝" back from the joint and centered on the tenon, with one exception: Each front-rail-to-front-leg joint has two evenly spaced counterbores, as shown here.*

Assembling the Seat

Rip and crosscut the seat slats (pieces 11 and 12), and make a bunch of ½"-thick spacers to set between the slats during the assembly. Working from back to front, put the pieces in place to see that they all fit, adjusting the spacer size if you aren't ending up with an even fit. The shorter slat fits between the front legs of the bench. Once you have a good fit, mark the slats for the counterbored pilot holes, and then remove them to rout all their edges with a ⅜" roundover bit. Sand the slats after routing the edges.

Slat Mortise Detail

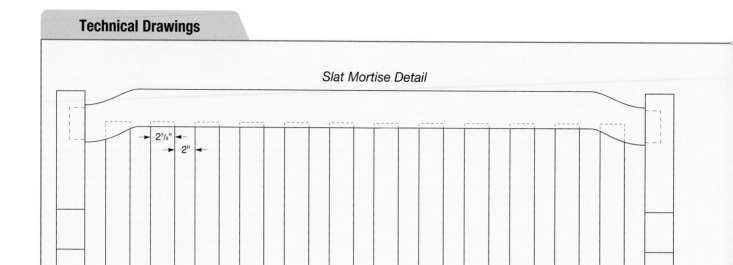

2³⁄₈"

2"

If you take a break now to apply your first coat of finish, you'll get better coverage and also avoid the headache of working around the installed seat slats. A true spar varnish is the best full-coating clear finish for outdoor use. Brush on a coat that has been thinned with about 10% mineral spirits for deeper penetration, and let it dry for a full 24 hours.

Replace the slats in the bench, and drill the counterbored pilot holes into the rails below (an angle drill is very handy for drilling under the arms). Now, drive in the #8-1¼" exterior screws (pieces 14), and then fill the counterbores with ⅜"-diameter white-oak plugs. Trim the plugs, sand them flush, and then give the entire bench a quick sanding with 220-grit sandpaper to remove the dust nibs. Next, apply at least two more coats of spar varnish at full strength to complete the project's weatherproofing.

Thoughts on Bench Care

When moving your bench outside, the first thing you'll notice is its heftiness. This project is built to last, and knowing that it has cross-pinned joints should make you even more confident of its longevity. Once you clear your eyes of the sweat produced during the big

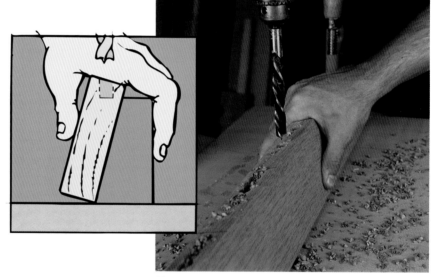

Figure 6: *Rip the face of your drill press fence at a 16° angle so it will hold the workpiece at that angle for properly drilling out the slat mortise waste in the back rail.*

move, the next thing you'll see is how well the bench complements your garden. If possible, keep the bench tucked under the overhanging leaves of an oak, out of direct sunlight and rain, and prop it off the ground to prevent rot from leaching up the legs. This will extend the time before the piece needs refinishing. Given this special care, your white-oak masterpiece will last at least as long as the venerable benches residing in English gardens.

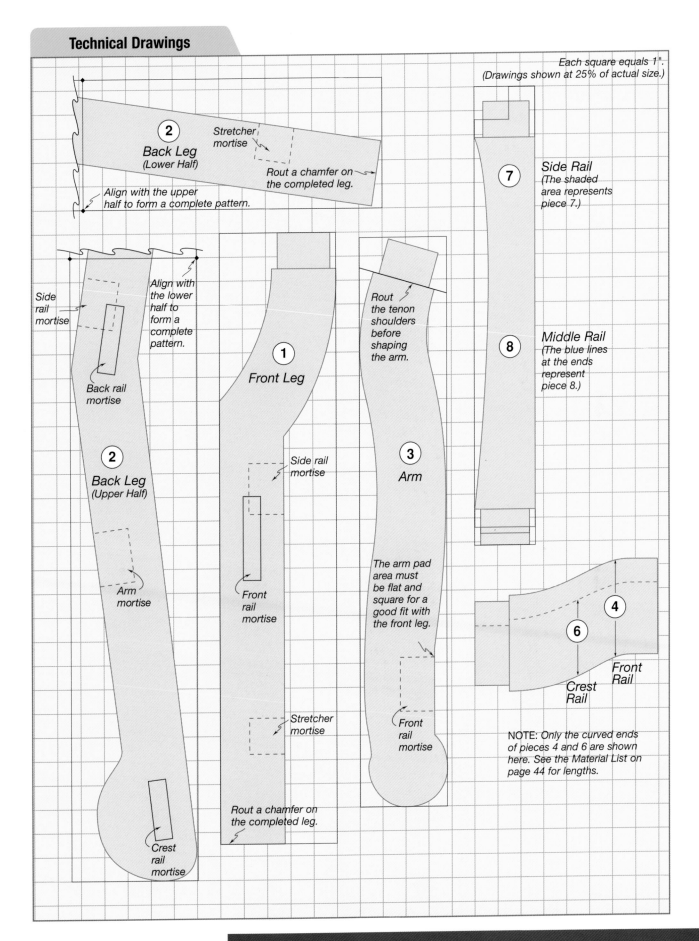

Each square equals 1".
(Drawings shown at 25% of actual size.)

②
Back Leg
(Lower Half)

Stretcher mortise

Rout a chamfer on the completed leg.

Align with the upper half to form a complete pattern.

Align with the lower half to form a complete pattern.

Side rail mortise

Back rail mortise

②
Back Leg
(Upper Half)

Arm mortise

Crest rail mortise

①
Front Leg

Side rail mortise

Front rail mortise

Stretcher mortise

Rout a chamfer on the completed leg.

Rout the tenon shoulders before shaping the arm.

③
Arm

The arm pad area must be flat and square for a good fit with the front leg.

Front rail mortise

⑦
Side Rail
(The shaded area represents piece 7.)

⑧
Middle Rail
(The blue lines at the ends represent piece 8.)

④

⑥

Crest Rail

Front Rail

NOTE: Only the curved ends of pieces 4 and 6 are shown here. See the Material List on page 44 for lengths.

Chairs

Rush-Covered Stool

This handsome rush-covered stool makes a distinctive accent piece in any entryway. It's also a fun way to learn some weaving skills you may not know and a chance to work with a medium other than wood. Enjoy the change!

by David Larson

My first experience working with rush came when I re-covered the seats on a set of flea-market chairs. First, I studied the original rush pattern, and then, after stripping and refinishing the wood parts of the chairs, I wove the new rush in exactly the same pattern. What an eye-opener! The weaving process—an age-old skill almost lost to Western designs these days—went quickly and seemed nearly foolproof to do successfully.

This small stool, which I built shortly after completing the chairs, demonstrates that rush weaving is not just for antiques. It adds dimension and an extra touch of comfort to what would otherwise be simply a well-built utility stool.

Figure 1: *A guide block with one end cut at 7° is a real help when paring the ends of the angled mortises.*

Laying the Groundwork

From the outset, I wanted this project to have enough flair to distinguish it from a run-of-the-mill store-bought stool. By laminating the rails and stretchers (pieces 1 through 6), and later cutting tapers on the legs (pieces 7), you'll create the kinds of distinctive details that make it clear that this stool is a handmade original.

Begin the project by cutting oversize ½"-thick cherry and ⅛"-thick walnut for gluing into the rail and stretcher laminations. Bear in mind that the laminations will be cut to size after the glue dries. Spread glue on all the mating surfaces, and after wiping off most of the glue squeeze-out,

leave the assemblies clamped overnight. The next time you come to the shop, joint one edge of each piece, and cut this stock to the sizes given in the Material List on page 55.

Most of the pieces in this project are shaped, but don't be too eager to band saw them at this early stage. Instead, cut as many joints as you can while the stock is still square, beginning with the mortises. Considering that some mortises are angled and others are square, the tool of choice for roughing all of them in is the drill press. Once you've bored the bulk of the waste out of each mortise, square up the ends and flatten the walls with a chisel.

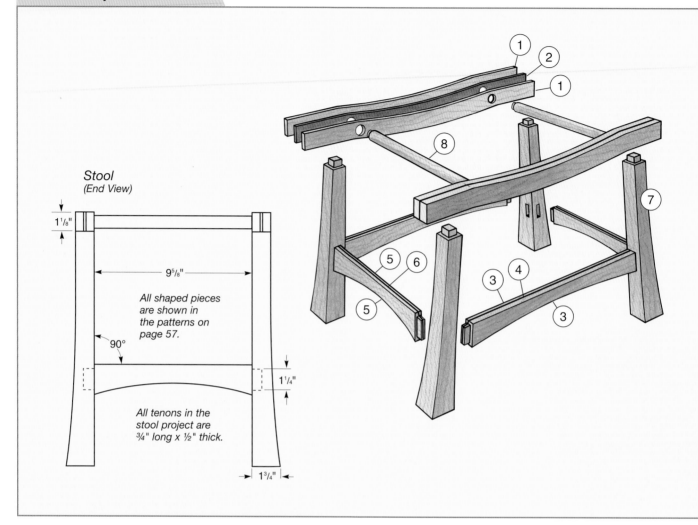

Stool
(End View)

1⅛"

9⅝"

90°

All shaped pieces
are shown in
the patterns on
page 57.

1¼"

All tenons in the
stool project are
¾" long x ½" thick.

1¾"

Figure 2: *To cut the square-shouldered tenons on the end stretchers, raise a ¾" dado blade ³⁄₁₆", and set the fence (with an auxiliary face) right next to the blade.*

Lay out the mortises on the rails, as shown in the rail pattern on page 57. Then, clamp a fence on your drill press table to center the bottom edge of the rail stock under a ½" brad-point or Forstner drill bit. Now, tilt your drill press table 7°, and bore 1⅝"-deep holes to hog out the mortise waste (double-check the entry angle to make sure it's correct for each mortise). Drilling these holes extradeep accounts for the waste that you'll cut away later when shaping the rails.

Once you've drilled the waste in the rail mortises, cut the legs to size, and lay out their mortises, as shown in the leg patterns on page 57. Drill the ¹³⁄₁₆"-deep angled mortises just as you did those on the rails. Then, reset your drill press table to 0°, and bore out the waste for the end stretcher mortises.

After the mortises have been roughed in, clean out the remaining waste with your chisels. One helpful trick I recommend for paring the ends of the angled mortises

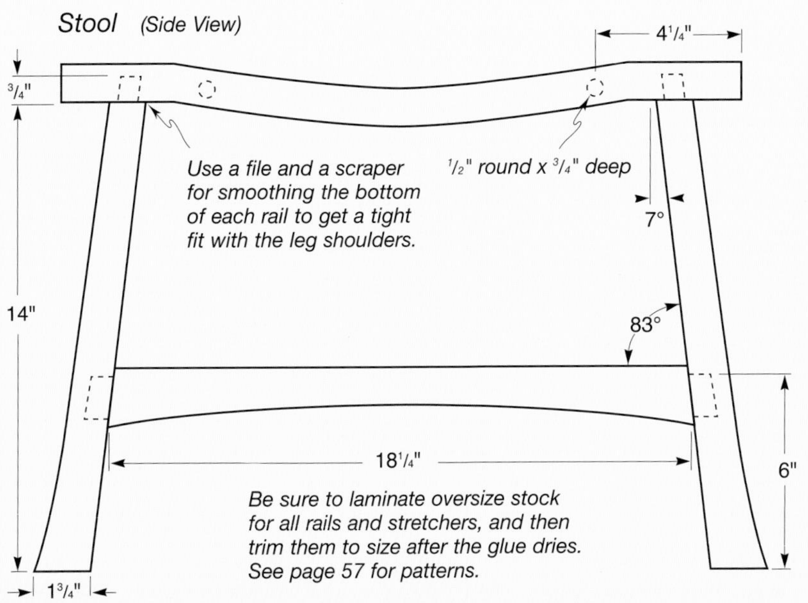

Stool (Side View)
4¼"
¾"
Use a file and a scraper for smoothing the bottom of each rail to get a tight fit with the leg shoulders.
½" round x ¾" deep
7°
14"
83°
18¼"
6"
Be sure to laminate oversize stock for all rails and stretchers, and then trim them to size after the glue dries. See page 57 for patterns.
1¾"

Material List

	T x W x L
1 Rail Laminations (4)	½" x 2" x 21"
2 Rail Laminations (2)*	⅛" x 2" x 21"
3 Side Stretcher Laminations (4)	½" x 2" x 19¾"
4 Side Stretcher Laminations (2)*	⅛" x 2" x 19¾"
5 End Stretcher Laminations (4)	½" x 2" x 11⅛"
6 End Stretcher Laminations (2)*	⅛" x 2" x 11⅛"
7 Legs (4)	1¾" x 1¾" x 14¾"
8 Support Dowels (2)	1" x 11⅛"
9 Rush (1)	400'

**Use walnut for pieces 2, 4, and 6.*

is to use a guide block to position the chisel at the correct angle (see Figure 1 on page 53). If you're a bit uncomfortable with hand tooling, make the angled guide block a few inches thick to provide almost total support behind the blade for making the angled chop cuts. This technique works great.

You'll notice that there's still a pair of mortises left to drill on the inside face of each rail for the support dowel joints (pieces 8). Lay out the drilling locations for the holes, as shown in the rail pattern, and then use your drill press to bore ½"-diameter x ¾"-deep holes. Fortunately, these holes need to remain round, so no chiseling is required.

Cutting the Tenons

As with the mortises in this stool, some of the tenon shoulders must be cut at a 7° angle, while others should be cut square. Cutting square-shouldered tenons on the end stretchers is a process you've probably done many times using a ¾" dado blade in your table saw (see Figure 2). Cutting the angled shoulders, however, may be less familiar. To make this process easy, build a crosscutting jig that rides in your table saw's miter gauge slot and has two fences angled 7° in opposite directions (see A Jig for Cutting Angled Tenons on page 56). The success of this jig depends on two things: The jig must be square to the blade, and the slope of the two fences must be exactly the same. I recommend that you set a bevel gauge to 7° and keep it at that setting throughout the project. This will provide a consistent reference for setting the fences and laying out the tenon shoulders. Once you've made the jig, run it through a ¾" dado blade so you can use the edge of the jig to align the tenon layouts with the blade.

Use the jig for cutting the side stretcher tenons first. Set the blade height, and place a stretcher against one of the jig fences. Align the shoulder layout line with the edge of the jig (make sure the slope of the layout line matches the angle of the cut), and screw a stop into the jig at the other end of the

A Jig for Cutting Angled Tenons

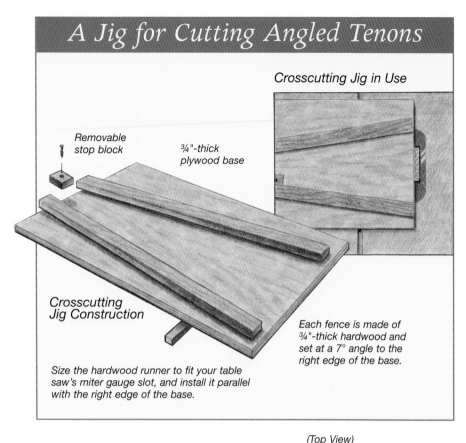

Crosscutting Jig in Use

Removable stop block

¾"-thick plywood base

Crosscutting Jig Construction

Size the hardwood runner to fit your table saw's miter gauge slot, and install it parallel with the right edge of the base.

Each fence is made of ¾"-thick hardwood and set at a 7° angle to the right edge of the base.

stretcher, as shown at left. Cut the first shoulder, turn the stretcher over, and cut an identical shoulder at the other end.

Repeat these steps on the second stretcher, and follow the same procedure for cutting the remaining shoulders with the second fence. Now, remove the stop block, and raise the blade to trim the tenon ends parallel with the shoulders. Since the side stretcher tenons will butt into the end stretcher tenons, miter their ends at 45°. Cut all the edge shoulders by hand.

Cutting a tenon on the end of each leg presents another challenge. Due to the taper on two sides of each leg (which you'll cut later), the tenon is situated near the inside corner of the leg rather than centered as usual. Consequently, the shoulder depths vary for each side of the tenons, as shown in the leg tenon detail drawings in Figure 3.

Lay out the leg tenons, label the depth of each shoulder cut, and then set the blade accordingly when you make the shoulder cuts. In all other respects, follow the same procedure for cutting these shoulders as you did for the stretchers.

Making Round Tenons

Forming ½"-round tenons on the ends of the support dowels is a safer job for the router table than for the table saw. Chuck a ½" straight bit in the router table, and clamp the fence ¼" from the bit. Now, slide your stock into the bit while keeping it in contact with the fence. Slowly spin the dowel to cut

Leg Tenon Detail

(Top View)

5/16" 1/2" 15/16"
3/16"
3/4"
13/16"

Figure 3: *When laying out the leg tenons, bear in mind that two sides of each leg will lose material during the tapering operation (shown in photo). To plan for this material loss, offset the tenon layout toward the inside corner of the leg, as shown in the top view of the leg tenon detail.*

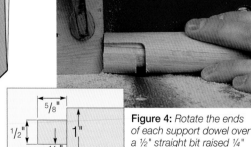

5/8"
1/2"
1/4"
1"

Figure 4: *Rotate the ends of each support dowel over a ½" straight bit raised ¼" to form round tenons with a router table.*

away the waste (see Figure 4), until it reaches the stop block. Make this cut with the bit set low at first, and then gradually reduce the tenon shape by raising the bit and making a couple more passes. Try this technique on an extra piece of 1"-diameter dowel first, until your sample tenon fits into the rail sockets just right.

Band Sawing the Shaped Pieces

All the joinery groundwork is now complete, and you're almost ready to start the assembly. But first, lay out the curves on the rails, stretchers, and legs, referring to the patterns at right, and band saw these pieces to shape. Then, drum sand the curves smooth, and use a file and scraper on the rails to get perfectly flat areas for the leg shoulders to bear against.

It's good protocol to put your projects through a dry assembly to make sure all the joints fit properly and to organize the clamps and other tools you'll need for the operation. With this project, first assemble the sides and then connect the two side assemblies with the end stretchers and support dowels. Breaking the assembly up like this makes it much more manageable.

Providing that all went well during the dry assembly, glue the stool together in the same order. Slice off any glue squeeze-out when it dries to a rubbery consistency, and then sand the stool with 150-grit sandpaper. I finished this stool with three coats of Watco Natural Oil and then rubbed on a coat of paste wax for good measure.

What's left to do? Weaving the rush (piece 9), of course. The process is described in Rush Weaving: A Step-by-Step Primer on page 58. Work your way through the process, which takes a couple of hours, and then apply oil-based walnut stain and two coats of varnish to the rush. When it's all done, you'll have a sturdy utility stool and some new skills for rehabilitating your own flea-market treasures.

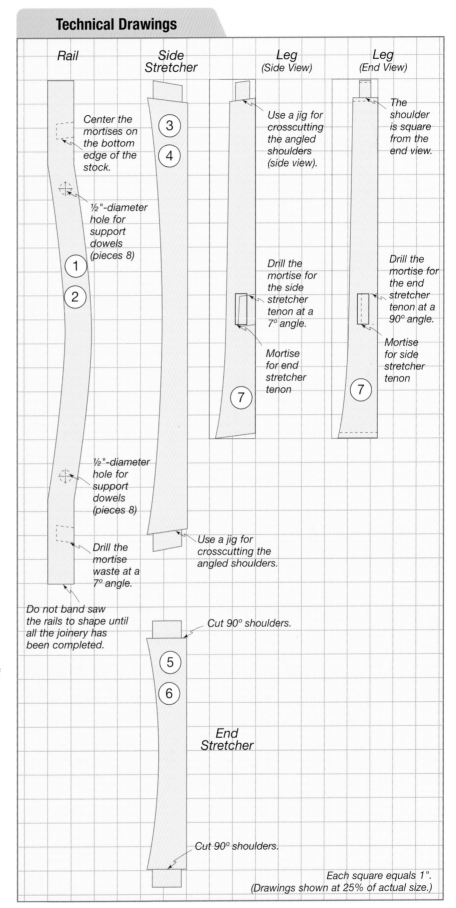

Technical Drawings

Rail

Center the mortises on the bottom edge of the stock.

½"-diameter hole for support dowels (pieces 8)

① ②

½"-diameter hole for support dowels (pieces 8)

Drill the mortise waste at a 7° angle.

Do not band saw the rails to shape until all the joinery has been completed.

Side Stretcher

③ ④

Use a jig for crosscutting the angled shoulders.

Leg (Side View)

Use a jig for crosscutting the angled shoulders (side view).

Drill the mortise for the side stretcher tenon at a 7° angle.

Mortise for end stretcher tenon

⑦

Leg (End View)

The shoulder is square from the end view.

Drill the mortise for the end stretcher tenon at a 90° angle.

Mortise for side stretcher tenon

⑦

Cut 90° shoulders.

⑤ ⑥

End Stretcher

Cut 90° shoulders.

Each square equals 1".
(Drawings shown at 25% of actual size.)

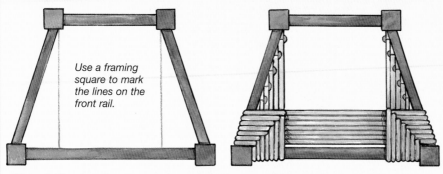

Use a framing square to mark the lines on the front rail.

Figure 1: *To square the weave, make marks on the front rail that are aligned with the ends of the back rail (left), and then weave individual strands of rush until you reach the marks (right), filling in the front corners of the seat as you go.*

As with so many woodworking firsts, the use of rush for seat coverings dates back to the time of the Egyptian pharaohs, around 4000 BC. For thousands of years, plants such as cattails, bulrush, and marsh flag have been harvested for making natural rush. Although these harvests continue today, natural rush has largely been replaced by fiber rush, which was developed in the early twentieth century.

Fiber rush is a tough, resilient product made of tightly twisted paper. It's easier to work than natural rush, comes in tremendously long strands, and is regarded as the most appropriate choice for the beginner. Of the five thicknesses in which fiber rush is available, the $\frac{5}{32}$" size is best for general work. To imitate the look of natural rush, fiber rush is available in a variegated cord containing brown, yellow, and green paper. This type of rush, along with the popular golden yellow variety, is the most durable; kraft brown rush is the least durable. When buying material, it's good to know that 2 pounds, or 400', of $\frac{5}{32}$" rush will cover an average chair, but only experience will tell you how much you'll need for a specific project.

Squaring the Weave

The key to weaving rush is to have a seat area that's as close to a square or a rectangle as possible. With the Rush-Covered Stool project featured on page 53, this is easily accomplished because the seat is built in a rectangle. The seat of a standard chair, however, is typically wider at the front than at the back. To weave this kind of flared seat, the first order of business is filling in the outside triangles—a process called squaring the weave.

To begin squaring the weave, draw lines on the front rail that are square with the ends of the back rail, as shown in Figure 1. These lines mark the inside edges of the imaginary triangles and the points at which you can stop the squaring weave. Start by tacking the end of a 10'-long rush strand to the left side rail about 2" from the leg, and then begin your weave. Go over and around the front rail, and then over and under the side rail (the same side rail the tack is driven into). Next, pull the rush across the chair to go over and around the opposite side rail, and then over and under the front rail. Tack the end of the strand to the right side rail 2" back from the leg, and cut off the excess.

Continue the squaring process by tacking a second strand to the left side rail just behind the first, and then repeating the same weave pattern. Weave as many strands as necessary to reach the lines on the front rail, making sure all the strands are spaced uniformly and pulled tight, as shown in Figure 1.

Starting the Stool

Once you've squared the weave, most rush projects are essentially the same. Before you actually begin weaving the stool seat, score the bottom of the stool's curved rails with a file or simply apply double-sided carpet tape, as shown in Figure 2. The extra gripping action gained by filing the rail or adding tape keeps the rush from slipping during the weaving process and later when someone is seated on the stool.

Cut about 25' of rush from your spool, and tack one end to a side rail a few inches inside the leg, as shown in Figure 2 (or next to the last of the squaring strands on a chair). Strands more than 25' long are difficult to handle and often become tangled. If the rush is a little stiff, moisten it with a mister to make it more manageable.

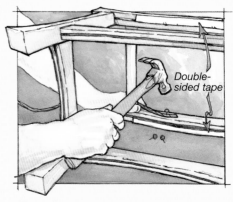

Double-sided tape

Figure 2

Begin weaving the stool seat by wrapping the strand over and around the nearest end rail, and then around the side rail, as shown in Figure 3. After completing the first course, press the rush tightly into the corners with a small wood wedge, and pull the strand taut.

Weave a second course right next to the first, and tighten it with the wedge. Then, weave a third course and so on, until you reach the end of the strand. As you tighten the strand, avoid

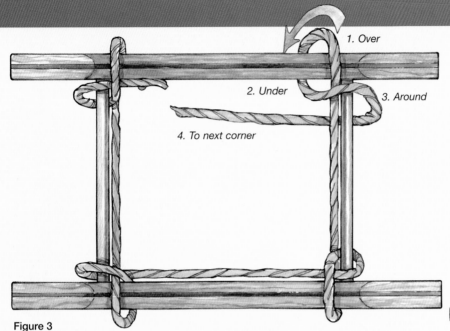

1. Over

2. Under

3. Around

4. To next corner

Figure 3

overlapping or crushing the rush in the corners, and take care to keep the weave square. Try not to tear the rush, but if a tear does occur, remove the damaged section and tie in a new piece of rush.

When you reach the end of the strand, tie on a new 25' piece with a square knot, making sure to pull the knot tight. A spring clamp is useful for holding the end of the woven strand tight while tying on the new piece of rush. Position all the knots well away from the corners so they won't interfere with the weave, as shown in Figure 4. But don't worry about the knots showing, because the corner weaves will eventually cover all of them.

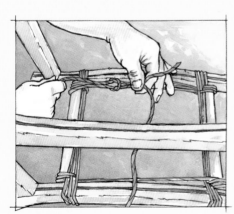

Figure 4

Stuffing the Weave

To give a rush seat more loft and make it more comfortable, slip corrugated cardboard between the layers in the weave (keep the corrugation lines running parallel with the adjacent rail).

Figure 5

Begin inserting the cardboard when you've woven about one-half to two-thirds of the seat area.

Cut eight triangular cardboard pieces to fit into the weave, as shown in Figure 5 (clip the leading point off each piece so it won't interfere with the weave as you reach the center of the stool). Working with the stool upside down, slip a cardboard piece into each weave section; then, turn the stool over, and install the other four pieces. Make the next eight cardboard triangles a little smaller, install them the same

way, and then make the next ones smaller yet. Continue adding cardboard until the weave looks even and the strands are pulled tight. Then, continue weaving the seat, but make sure you can finish with one length of rush—a knot is difficult to hide at this stage.

Once you've covered two of the rails with rush, stop working around the seat from corner to corner, and switch to a figure-eight weave, as shown in Figure 6. Start with the strand going over one rail to the middle of the chair, and then slip it through the weave and

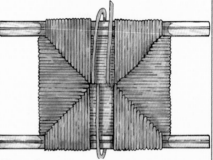

Figure 6

underneath the seat to the opposite rail. Reverse the weave back to the first rail to complete one figure eight. Follow this pattern to complete the seat. Then, tack the strand to a rail, and tuck a few inches of excess into the weave, as shown in Figure 7.

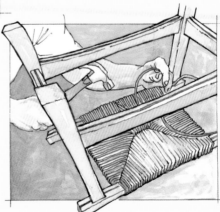

Figure 7

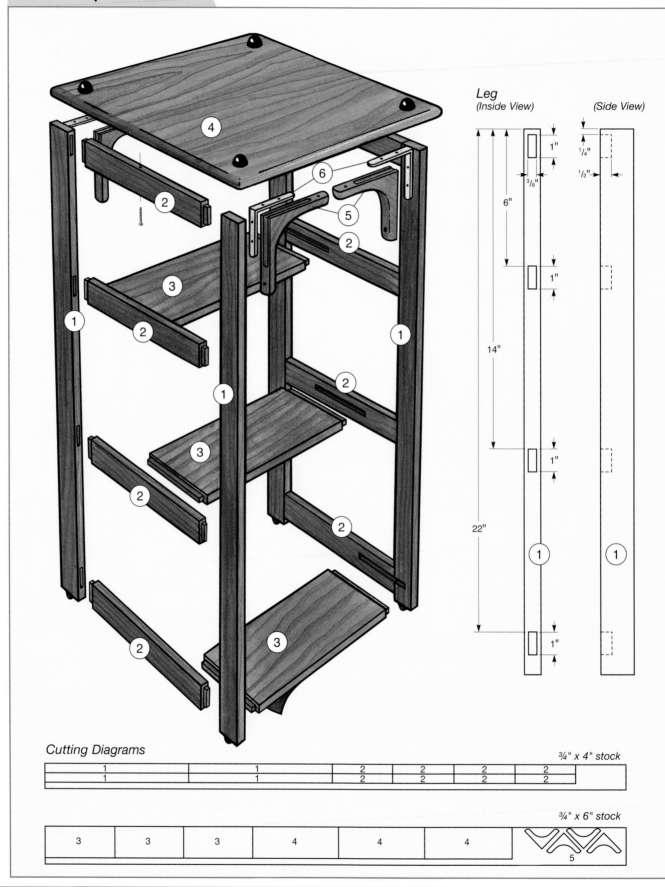

Leg
(Inside View)　　　　(Side View)

Cutting Diagrams

¾" x 4" stock

| 1 | | 1 | 2 | 2 | 2 | 2 | |
| 1 | | 1 | 2 | 2 | 2 | 2 | |

¾" x 6" stock

| 3 | 3 | 3 | 4 | 4 | 4 | |

Stretcher (Top View)

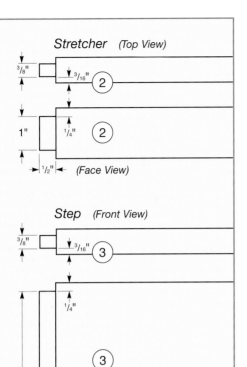

3/8"
3/16"
(2)

1"
1/4"
(2)
1/2"
(Face View)

Step (Front View)

3/8"
3/16"
(3)

1/4"

4 1/2"
(3)

1/2"
(Top View)

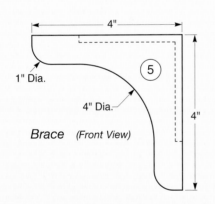

4"
1" Dia.
(5)
4" Dia.
4"

Brace (Front View)

Material List

	T x W x L
1 Legs (4)	¾" x 1½" x 23⅞"
2 Stretchers (8)	¾" x 1½" x 10"
3 Steps (3)	¾" x 5" x 11½"
4 Seat (1)	¾" x 14" x 14"
5 Braces (4)	¾" x 4" x 4"
6 L-Brackets (4)	Steel

Figure 1: *Begin making the mortises by boring out the waste using a sharp Forstner bit. All you need to locate the mortise is a centerline and two cross-marks indicating the ends of the mortise.*

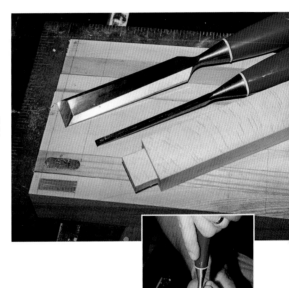

Figure 2: *Pare the walls of the mortise smooth and flat with a couple of sharp chisels. It's best to make the mortises first and then form tenons to fit the openings.*

Figure 3: *Ash lumber is easier to pare than oak, and it is more than sufficiently strong for this step stool's rigorous daily tasks.*

Machining Details

I followed the usual convention of making mortises first and then tenons to fit them. Use a ⅜" Forstner bit chucked in your drill press to remove the bulk of the waste. Lay out each mortise with a simple centerline and cross-marks to indicate its ends. Then, hog out the waste, spacing the holes a bit's width apart (see Figure 1). Once you've reached the other end of the mortise, drill away the remaining waste. This staggering procedure helps prevent the drill bit from bending.

The next step is to square up the mortises with chisels (see Figure 2). This is another place where the choice of ash over oak is a benefit. If your chisel is sharp, it will cut through ash like a hot knife through butter (see Figure 3).

The tenons are easy to form since they can all be cut from a single setup on the table saw. The shoulders and cheeks are all ⅜" wide. Set up a stacked dado blade with a sacrificial board fastened tight to the rip fence. Use some scrap wood (cut to the same dimensions as your project stock) to fine-tune your setup until the tenons fit snug, but not overly tight. Then, cut tenons on all the stretchers and steps.

You will need to drill a pilot hole in each of the top stretchers to mount the seat (see the drawing on page 62). After assembly, a conventional drill will not fit between the stretchers, so use your drill press now to bore a ³⁄₁₆" through hole in the exact center of the ¾" face. Then, finish up these holes with an appropriate countersink.

Beginning Assembly

Assembling the stool is pretty much woodworking by the numbers, but you don't want to get ahead of yourself. Start by gluing up the two side assemblies, checking that all the faces are as flush as possible and that the countersinks in the top stretchers are on the inside of the frame, facing up. Clamp the assemblies, check them for square, and set them aside to allow the glue to fully cure.

While you have a moment, now is a good time to cut the seat to its final size, radius its corners to 1", and sand its edges smooth all around. To add visual appeal and to make the seat a bit more comfortable, the top edge is milled with a ½" roundover bit and the bottom edge with a ¼" roundover. All that's left to be done on the seat is to give it a final sanding and, of course, apply the finish.

Once the side assemblies are dry, they each need three mortises cut to accommodate the steps. You can either carefully mark and hand cut these, or you can make a template and mill them with a router (see A Template for Routing Mortises on page 65). Be sure to flip the template over when doing the second side assembly. They must be mirror images of each other.

Creating Clever Corners

The original stool had oak corner braces to help mount the seat. I made the braces (pieces 5) from the remainder of my 6" board, as shown in the cutting diagram on page 62. Now, round over the braces, sand them, and drill countersunk mounting holes in them. Because of the hard use this stool will take, add steel L-brackets (pieces 6) to reinforce the joints. To keep the brackets from showing, undercut or rout out the inside edges of the wood braces, and screw them in place over the steel brackets. Do this on your router table, as shown in Figure 4.

With the pieces prepared for final assembly, it's a good idea to prefinish the parts. All the corners and possible

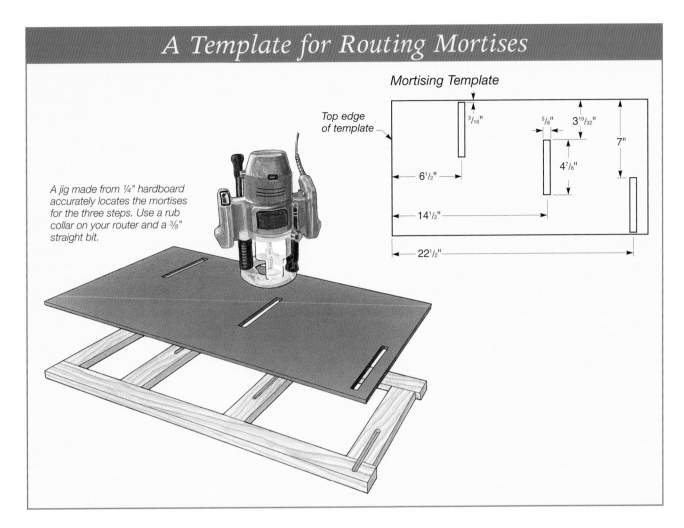

Mortising Template

Top edge of template

A jig made from ¼" hardboard accurately locates the mortises for the three steps. Use a rub collar on your router and a ⅜" straight bit.

³/₁₆"   ⁵/₈"   3¹⁹/₃₂"   7"

4⁷/₈"

6½"

14½"

22½"

glue lines will be more difficult to work with if you stain the stool after assembly. Be sure to mask off the tenons and mortises, or your joints will not glue well.

Finally, the stool is beginning to take shape. Glue the steps in place, and clamp the frame together. Do this on a dead-even surface.

Set the seat facedown on the workbench, and center the frame on top. Secure the frame with 2" black finish screws, and attach the steel brackets with screws, as well. Then, mount the wood braces, which effectively hide the steel brackets.

Adding a Kitchen-Safe Finish

With the stool assembled, apply your topcoat. I used two coats of polyurethane, with a wax follow-up.

Once the finish is fully cured, the rubber treads (made from rubber carpet runners) can be added to the steps to improve footing. Cut them to size, and apply them with contact adhesive. Then, add the feet. The original stool had steel pronged feet, but I substituted rubber for the sake of safety. Attach one to each corner of the top about 1" in from the edges, and one to the center of each of the four feet.

This is a fun project to build. Its simple traditional joinery and basic cuts make it an excellent project for beginner and expert alike. Oh, and the original on eBay? It sold for a bit over $300! Why not take the extra money you would have spent and invest it on that next piece of shop machinery?

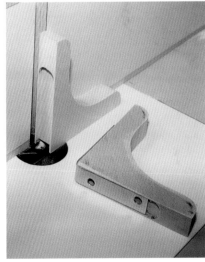

Figure 4: *To be sure the stool will stand up to the rigors of everyday use, mount steel L-brackets to the seat and legs. You can hide the hardware in the wood corner braces by routing a pocket in each.*

by Bruce Kieffer

Intarsia-Backed High Chair

Here's a project that accomplishes several wonderful purposes: It creates a sturdy, safe place to share meals with a youngster, and then it becomes a family heirloom that's sure to be passed down through many generations. It also provides an opportunity for you to try your hand at the ancient art of intarsia.

There's something about wooden high chairs that feels more inviting than their more prosaic plastic counterparts. And when you add Judy Gale Roberts' intarsia "Chowhound" to this chair, you also have a wonderful family heirloom. Intarsia is essentially a mosaic of different-colored woods cut into shapes and assembled to create an image. This design was created by renowned intarsist Judy Gale Roberts, and she tells you how to do it step-by-step beginning on page 76.

The chair is made from red oak and built like a tank, yet it doesn't look heavy. Its wide stance makes it very stable. I designed it to be easy to build. The hardest part of the construction process will be keeping track of which part is which, and which way the angled cuts are made. The legs and back posts have compound mitered ends, and they're mirror images of each other. To make it less confusing, label the legs and back posts as *right* and *left*, and label each part with *front*, *back*, *in*, *out*, *up*,

and *down*. That will help a lot, but you may also find it helpful to hold up the parts in the orientation they will have in the finished chair. That way, you can easily tell if you are about to goof up on the next cut. The lower stretchers, footrest, seat, arms, and back panel are all fit during assembly. This eliminates the need to be dead-on when cutting

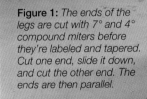

Figure 1: *The ends of the legs are cut with 7° and 4° compound miters before they're labeled and tapered. Cut one end, slide it down, and cut the other end. The ends are then parallel.*

Material List

	T x W x L			T x W x L
1 Front Legs (2)	1½" x 2³⁄₁₆" x 27⅛"		11 Crest Rail (1)	1⅛" x 4" x 12"
2 Back Legs (2)	1½" x 2" x 21¼"		12 Lower Back Rail (1)	1⅛" x 2" x 10⅜"
3 Front and Back Aprons (2)	¾" x 3" x 14⅛"		13 Back Panel** (1)	½" x 10" x 12"
4 Side Aprons (2)	¾" x 3" x 10⅞"		14 Arms (2)	¾" x 2¼" x 14½"
5 Side Stretchers* (2)	¾" x 1½" x 15"		15 Screw Plugs (6)	⅜" Dia. x ⅜"
6 Center Stretcher* (1)	¾" x 1" x 17"		16 Screw-On Slides (4)	⅞"-Dia. Nylon
7 Seat Cleats (2)	¾" x 1½" x 13¾"		17 Tray Hardware (2)	Steel
8 Footrest (1)	¾" x 3¼" x 16"		18 Oak Tray (1)	Red Oak
9 Seat** (1)	¾" x 15" x 17½"		19 Safety Straps (1)	Black Nylon
10 Back Posts (2)	1½" x 2" x 15⅜"			

*Cut to length.
**Oversize (see drawings and text for fabrication details).

Figure 2: *Use a band saw to cut the leg tapers. Cut just to the outside of the drawn lines. A wide band saw blade will make straighter cuts that require less sanding.*

the compound miters on the leg and back post ends, as well as the miters on the seat apron ends.

As I neared the end of the construction, I found it a bit difficult to fit the back panel. It's an odd shape and needs to fit well. What I ended up doing was making a template from scrap MDF (medium-density fiberboard). Once that fit, I used the template as a router guide to cut the final back panel. Enough said—let's make some dust!

Making Legs, Compound Miters, and Tapers

The leg ends are cut 7° front to back and 4° side to side (see the drawings on pages 74–75). Cutting these compound miters is most easily done before labeling and tapering the legs, using one setup. Then, you will visually orient the pieces the way they will be set when the chair is assembled, label them, cut the footrest dadoes, and make the tapers.

Cut the front and back legs (pieces 1 and 2) to the sizes given in the Material List, above. Set your power miter saw to cut a 7° miter and a 4° bevel. On each piece, cut one end, slide the leg across the saw's table, and cut the other end. That way, the end

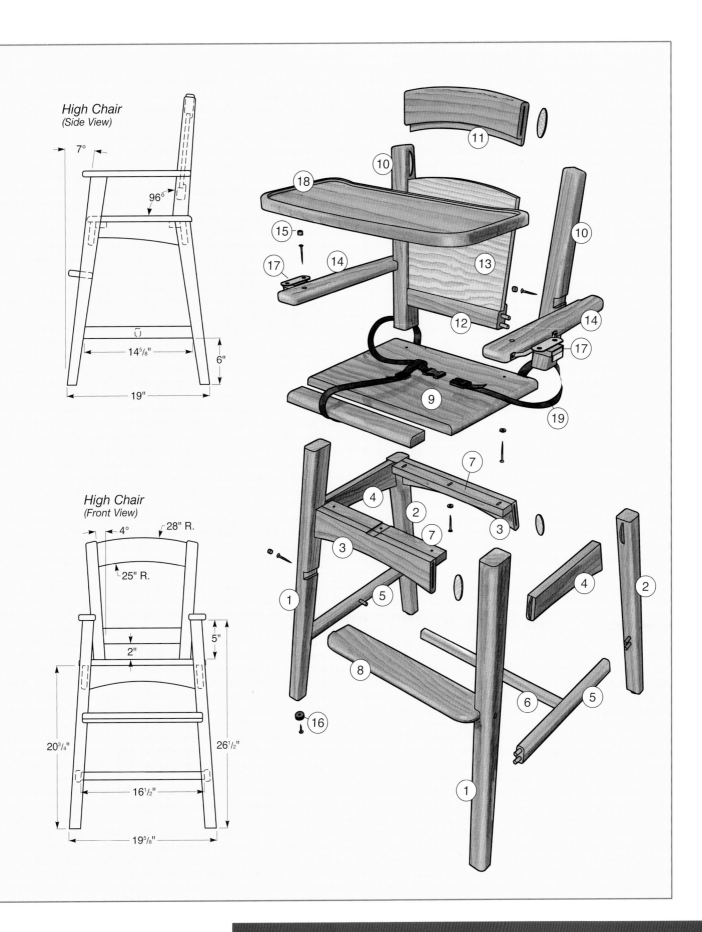

High Chair
(Side View)

7°

96°

14⁵⁄₈"

6"

19"

High Chair
(Front View)

4°

28" R.

25" R.

5"

2"

20³⁄₄"

26¹⁄₂"

16¹⁄₂"

19⁵⁄₈"

Figure 3: *Chop mortises for biscuits on the legs. Then, cut the biscuit grooves centered in the ends of the side aprons with a ⅜"-thick spacer placed under the joiner's fence. This creates the ⅜" offset.*

cuts are perfectly parallel (see Figure 1 on page 67).

Visually orient the legs, and then label them. Lay out the dadoes on the insides of the front legs for the footrest (piece 8). Mount a ¾" dado in your table saw, and angle the cut to 4° while setting the height to ¼". Use a miter gauge set at 90°, and cut the dadoes. Watch how you have the legs oriented on the miter gauge so you get the angles going the right way. One leg is cut with its bottom pointing right, and the other with its bottom pointing left.

Lay out the leg tapers, as shown in the drawings. Then, cut the tapers (see Figure 2 on page 68), and sand them smooth. Lay out and drill the footrest plug and screw holes in the front legs.

The work that remains to get the base assembled is fairly straightforward. I used a self-centering doweling jig to drill all of the base's dowel holes, making fast work of an otherwise tedious job. I also used spacers with a biscuit joiner to quickly align it when cutting the biscuit grooves

for the offset apron-to-leg joints (see Figure 3).

Cut the front and back aprons (pieces 3) and the side aprons (pieces 4) to the sizes given in the Material List. Step to your table saw to bevel the top edges of the front and back apron pieces 7° and the top edges of the side apron pieces 4°. Use your power miter saw to miter the ends of the front and back aprons at 4° and the ends of the side aprons at 9°. Lay out the gentle curves on the aprons, as shown in the drawings on page 75, and cut them.

Locate and cut the apron-to-leg biscuit joints. Use the back legs to find the height of the apron pieces on the front legs. Remember that the biscuits that join the side aprons to the front legs are #0s, and the rest are #20s. The side aprons are set back ⅜" from the outsides of the legs, and the front and back aprons are held back ¾" from the nontapered edges of the legs.

Cut the side and center stretchers (pieces 5 and 6) to size, but leave them a bit long. Dry fit the front legs,

back legs, and side aprons together as two separate side assemblies. Miter the ends of the side stretchers to 9°, slowly nibbling away at their lengths until they fit between the front and back legs. Mark where the ends of the side stretchers land on the insides of the legs. Dismantle the dry-assembled base sides. Lay out and drill the leg-to-side-stretcher dowel holes. Now, dry assemble the entire base, and fit the center stretcher just as you did the side stretchers. When it fits properly, dismantle the base completely, and lay out and drill dowel holes to join the center stretcher and side stretchers.

Rout the large roundovers on the outside edges of the legs and the smaller radius on the legs, aprons, and stretchers (see the drawings on page 69). When rounding over the front legs, be careful to keep the bit's bearing from falling into the footrest dadoes and screw plug holes, or you'll mess up the front legs in a hurry!

Make and attach the seat cleats (pieces 7). The edges that join with the front and back aprons are cut at a 7° bevel, and the screw holes in the back seat cleat are elongated to allow for movement of the seat.

Finish sand the base parts. Glue and clamp the legs, side aprons, and side stretchers together to make the base side subassemblies. When these assemblies have dried, glue and clamp them together with the front and back aprons and center stretcher. Use a flat surface so the chair won't rock after it's assembled (see Figure 4).

Rout or chop a groove for the front center seat safety strap on the top of the front apron and seat cleat, checking that the strap fits well in its groove.

Making the Seat

The seat is made large to begin with so you can cut off and fit the front edge between the front legs and then reattach that piece. This is much easier than trying to hand cut angled notches on the seat's front corners.

Make the seat (piece 9) by edge gluing three boards together and then cutting it to size after the glue has cured. Slice 1¾" off its front edge at a 9° bevel (see the drawing on page 75). Bevel the ends of this piece 4° so it fits between the front legs. Edge glue the seat front piece back onto the seat blank, flush and centered. Set the seat on the base, and mark it to cut the final shape of the

seat (see the drawing on page 69). Cut the shape, radius the back corners, rout the ½"-radius roundover edges, and finish sand the seat.

Forming the Back Frame

Next, cut the back posts (pieces 10) to size. Cutting the ends of the back posts is a little different from doing the legs. Miter the bottom ends with a 6° miter and a 4° bevel. With these settings, cut one back post end with that back post to the left of the saw blade, and cut the other back post end with that back post to the right of the saw blade. Visually orient the back posts, and label them. Then, lay out and cut the 8° bevels on the top ends.

Figure 4: *Glue and clamp the base parts together on a flat surface. Laying a board across the tops of the side and front aprons will ensure that the front apron is at the proper height.*

Crest Rail
(Front and End Views)

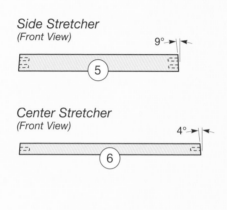

12"

28" R.

(11)

25" R.

4°

1 1/8"

3"

1/2"

3/8"

Lower Back Rail
(Front and End Views)

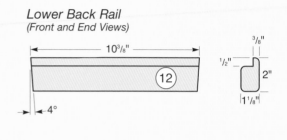

10 3/8"

(12)

4°

3/8"

1/2"

2"

1 1/8"

Side Stretcher
(Front View)

9°

(5)

Center Stretcher
(Front View)

4°

(6)

Front Leg

(Front View)   (Inside View)

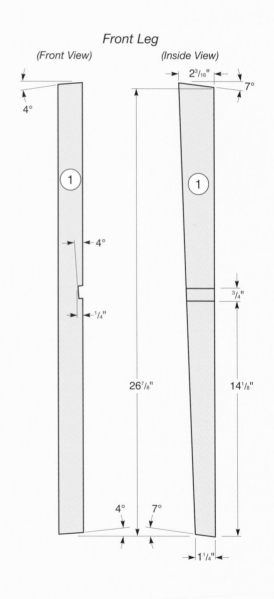

2 3/16"

7°

4°

(1)   (1)

4°

3/4"

1/4"

26 7/8"   14 1/8"

4°   7°

1 1/4"

Back Post

(Side View)   (Front View)

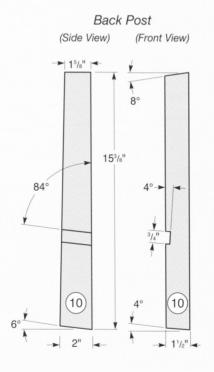

1 5/8"

8°

15 3/8"

84°

4°

3/4"

(10)   (10)

6°   4°

2"   1 1/2"

NOTE: The outside edges of the legs and back posts (pieces 1, 2, and 10) are formed with a ½" roundover, as are the top edges of the seat (piece 9). All other roundovers are ¼". The rear corners of the seat are ½" radii.

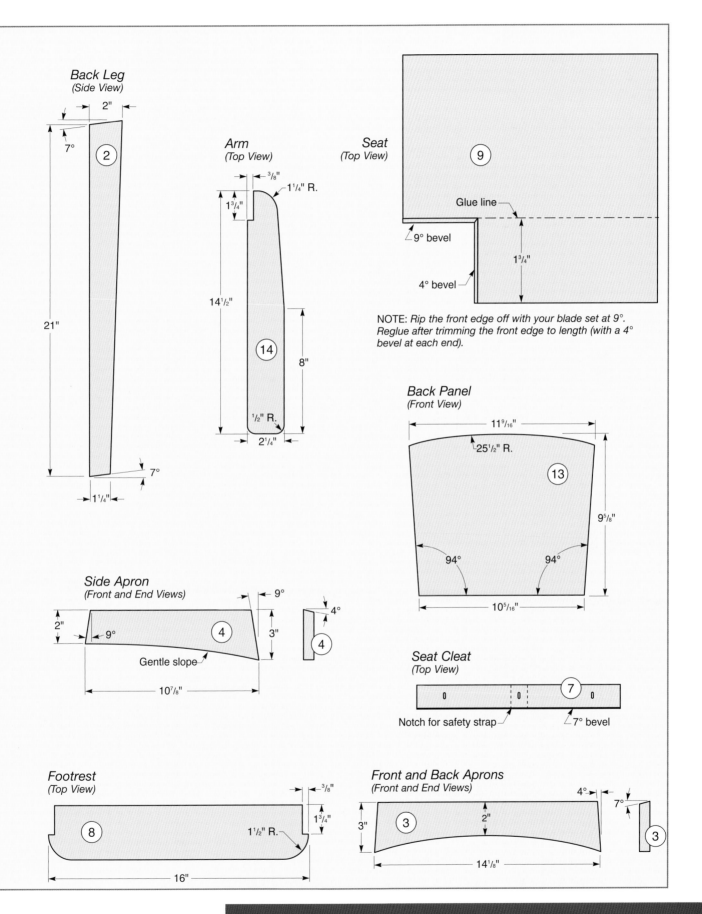

Back Leg
(Side View)

2"

7°

②

21"

7°

1 1/4"

Arm
(Top View)

3/8"

1 1/4" R.

1 3/4"

14 1/2"

⑭

8"

1/2" R.

2 1/4"

Seat
(Top View)

⑨

Glue line

9° bevel

4° bevel

1 3/4"

NOTE: *Rip the front edge off with your blade set at 9°. Reglue after trimming the front edge to length (with a 4° bevel at each end).*

Back Panel
(Front View)

11 9/16"

25 1/2" R.

⑬

9 5/8"

94°   94°

10 5/16"

Side Apron
(Front and End Views)

9°

2"

9°

④

3"

4°

④

Gentle slope

10 7/8"

Seat Cleat
(Top View)

0   0   ⑦   0

Notch for safety strap   7° bevel

Footrest
(Top View)

3/8"

1 3/4"

⑧

1 1/2" R.

16"

Front and Back Aprons
(Front and End Views)

4°

7°

3"

③

2"

③

14 1/8"

Intarsia is a mosaic of different colors and species of wood that are carefully cut and put together to create a picture.

Judy Gale Roberts has been creating intarsia patterns for more than 25 years, and she has more than 10 books on the subject to her credit, including *Easy to Make Inlay Wood Projects* and *Intarsia Workbook*, both available from Fox Chapel Publishing (*www.foxchapelpublishing.com*). Sometimes her ideas are inspired by wood grain; other times it will be a specific "prize board." Her background is in sculpture (ceramic, metal, and mixed media), and she greatly enjoys the sculptural aspect of intarsia. "The wood comes to life when you start shaping each part," Judy says.

Judy works in partnership with her husband, Jerry Booher. They offer a free intarsia newsletter with more than 225 patterns, available by calling 800-316-9010 or by e-mailing *jerry@intarsia.com*.

For Judy's "chowhound" intarsia, use a copy machine to enlarge the pattern on page 78, and make multiple copies. Then, cut the pattern pieces apart, and attach them to the wood. The arrows indicate grain direction. Cut the pieces out on your scroll saw, cutting directly on the line. (Note: Do not sand to fit, because you risk sanding the sides at an angle that will cause problems when you begin shaping the project.) After cutting out the pieces, leave the paper on, and assemble the parts into a whole picture. If there is a lot of the line left and the project isn't fitting, put a new blade in your scroll saw and trim to fit on the scroll saw.

Once the pieces are fitting into the pattern, remove the paper. Number the parts by writing the number on the back side of each piece of wood—this will help to keep you from shaping the wrong side of a piece.

Using a spindle sander to round the edges of each piece of the pup will give the intarsia a quilt-like appearance and make things more comfortable for the child in the high chair.

After shaping the pieces, apply three coats of finish, but leave the bottom of each piece finish free. Apply the finish to each part individually in case you need to sand between coats, making it easier to sand with the grain. Let the finish dry, and then glue the intarsia down.

Judy Gale Roberts is a true intarsia artist and the author of many books on the subject. Judy is credited for much of the renewed interest in the ancient art of intarsia.

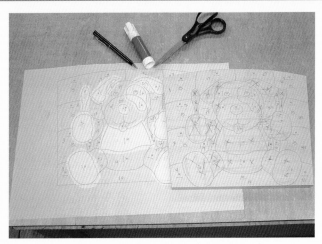

Step 1: *Make several copies of the pattern. Cut out each piece with scissors. Gluing one copy of the intact pattern to a piece of ¼" hardboard will come in handy later, during the assembly of all the pieces.*

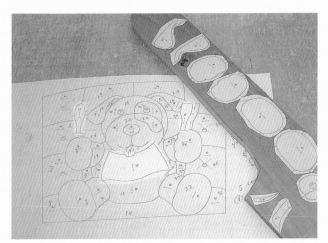

Step 2: *Glue the cutout pattern pieces to selected chunks of wood. Take note of the arrows that indicate grain direction. The direction and figure of the grain provide depth and texture in the finished piece.*

Step 4: *With all the parts numbered on their back faces, remove the paper, and examine how the parts fit together. If necessary, this is the time to make a new piece to create just the look you are after.*

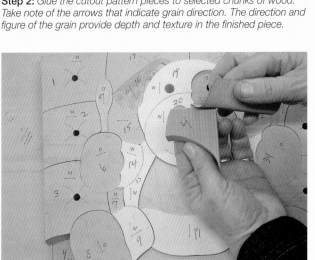

Step 3: *Dry fit the parts together. Number your master copy of the pattern (seen below the wooden pieces), and transfer the numbers to the backs of the cutout pieces. Carefully fit them together.*

Step 5: *Gently break the edges of the pieces to create a quilt-like effect. Remember to be consistent—there are lots of pieces to shape, and they will be viewed in relationship to each other.*

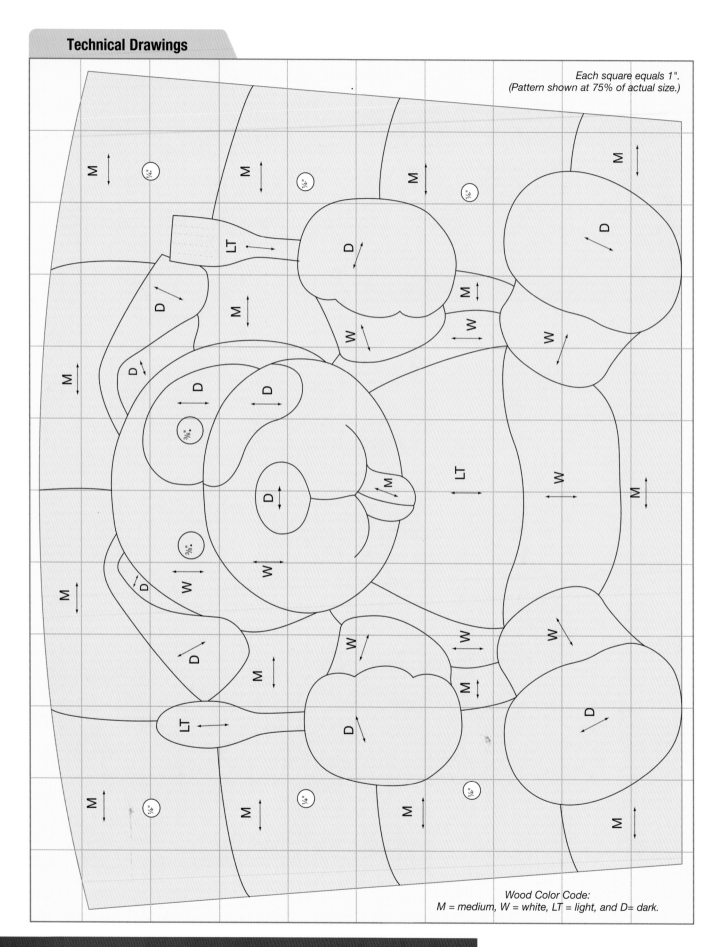

Each square equals 1".
(Pattern shown at 75% of actual size.)

Wood Color Code:
M = medium, W = white, LT = light, and D= dark.

A Brief History of the
Adirondack Chair

Learn the origins of this enduring American archetype.

by Rob Johnstone

The new century was blooming warm and beautiful on the shores of Lake Champlain, New York, in the summer of 1902. At the family vacation house (dubbed Stony Sides), Thomas Lee was confronting a problem. Lee thought that he, and the nearly 22 relatives vacationing with him in the Adirondack Mountains, might benefit from some comfortable outdoor seating. So, grabbing a hammer, nails, and some wide pine boards, Lee walked out to the front lawn and began making a series of chairs—prototypes with slanting backs and wide armrests—with each and every new attempt being evaluated by his oh-so-many relatives.

Their unvarnished feedback led to more and more efforts at outdoor seating perfection. The records are unclear as to the exact number of attempts, but with 22 different opinions, not to mention derrieres, to please, one can only guess that there were many. Likewise, one has to wonder whether the final version was the result of universal acceptance or builder's exhaustion.

In any case, Lee built several chairs, and they were well received that summer by family and friends. They were all constructed with a single wide board as the back—undoubtedly made from old-growth white-pine lumber, which was plentiful in the area. The angles and armrests of those original chairs would be entirely familiar to us today: Painted brown or green, the chairs eventually became part of the American landscape. But the story could easily have ended back in 1902, for Lee had no broader ambitions for his invention than the confines of Stony Sides' lawns—a gracious expanse, but a limited scope. Then, as they say, the plot thickened.

In the tiny nearby town of Westport, an impoverished friend of Lee's by the name of Harry Bunnell, a carpenter by trade, desperately needed to generate some income during the long New York winter. Lee, proud of his summertime invention, kindly gave the design to Bunnell, as something he might build over the winter

The classic Adirondack chair profile is unmistakable in this 1905 "Westy."

and sell to vacationers in the summer. Bunnell immediately saw the potential of the chair and started production.

Bunnell also, apparently without Lee's permission, submitted and received a patent on the "Westport Chair" around 1905. "The object of this invention," wrote Bunnell, "is a chair of the bungalow type adapted for use on porches, lawns, and at camps and also adapted to be converted into an invalid's chair."

Harry Bunnell continued to build the Westport chair, and variations on its theme, for the next 20 years. The popularity of the chairs, and the success of Thomas Lee's design, was simply remarkable.

As the design's popularity waxed, the name Adirondack chair became synonymous with Westport chair. As the chair migrated into Canada, it gained the sobriquet of the Muskokas chair, most significantly in the Big Three Lakes region of Ontario. At the turn of the last century, an original Westport chair would have sold for around $4 (perhaps less). Today, that same chair, in good condition, might command as much as $1,250.

Adirondack Chair Revisited

Here's a charming hardwood version of an American classic, recreated after the style of Greene and Greene. Inspired by a beautiful garden gate, it's a sophisticated design that's solidly built and comfortable, as well.

by Dana and Michael Van Pelt

As admirers of Charles and Henry Greene's architectural and interior furnishing designs, we decided to search the exteriors of the historic Greene and Greene homes for a hint of the brothers' well-known style in the lawn and garden furnishings there—with no luck. We found built-in benches and lawns adorned with traditional Adirondack chairs and wicker furniture, but that was about as close as we got.

Desiring an outdoor furniture style that would complement a Greene and Greene home, we created the chair presented here. It adds the California spirit of the brothers' design sense to the sensible "Yankee" Adirondack chair.

When you think about it, a Greene and Greene–style Adirondack chair sounds almost like an oxymoron (think "sanitary sewer" or "organized political party"). But, in fact, when we combined the two styles, we ended up with a sophisticated design that promised to deliver comfortable summertime seating.

As luck would have it, the beautiful garden gate at the Greene brothers' Thorsen house provided the perfect inspiration for the design. The pattern of the Thorsen gate is a clever interplay of positive and negative space, of curves and straight lines. We successfully transferred those forms to this chair's back slats. The two sides of the back mirror one another as they follow along the center piece, curving with the organic lines that are so in keeping with the Greene brothers' vision. The center piece captures two routed openings, which provide the negative space (see Figure 1).

Where straight, hard lines would be found in a traditional Adirondack chair, such as on the arms, legs, and stretchers, we employed slight curves to better reflect the Greene and Greene philosophy. Many Adirondack chairs' arm supports and legs stand flat and perpendicular to the seat and lounging leg. We modified this approach by rotating the front leg 90° to the lounging leg, giving the arm extra strength as it captures the leg in its open-ended dado.

The horizontal stretchers and supports reflect elements of the Asian-inspired "cloud lift" (a slight elevation in the lines), a design often found in the Greenes' masterworks. The seat slats are spaced evenly and secured into place with screw fasteners, with the holes then plugged to hide the screws.

To further evoke the Greene and Greene essence, we wanted to mimic the ebony accents that are so often seen in their furniture pieces. We used ebony epoxy for the stylish detail plugs—confident that the epoxy would tolerate adverse weather and the beating of the sun.

We decided to use mahogany hardwood (a full 1" thick), which is typical of the wood used by the Greene brothers in their furniture construction. As this is an outdoor project, you could choose other material, as well. Lyptus, a new hybrid lumber on the market, would work well, as would the old standby, teak—just be sure that it's plantation grown if you go that route. We would recommend staying away from cedar and redwood, but cypress would be a nice softwood alternative.

Figure 1: *The design of this chair's back slats was inspired by the garden gate of the Greene brothers–designed Thorsen house.*

Making Templates

Take a look at the Material List on page 83. For the pieces listed there, it gives the proper dimensions to use with the pattern drawings provided on pages 84–85. Enlarge the patterns to full-size, and make hardboard or plywood templates of the pieces for best results. You'll then transfer the shapes to your stock by tracing around your templates (see Figure 2). And be sure you save the templates to make additional chairs.

Figure 2: *Create templates of the shaped parts from the patterns. Use the templates to transfer the shapes to each piece as needed.*

Beginning the Foundation

Start by making the arms (pieces 1). Trace the arm pattern onto the stock, and then lay out the stopped dado on its lower face. Before you shape this piece on the band saw, mill the stopped dado using a router and a ¾" straight bit. Use a clamped-on straightedge to guide your cut.

Next, mill the back arm support and the front legs (pieces 2 and 3). Note that the arm support has one 30° edge. After transferring these shapes to the wood, cut out their forms—along with the arms that you started above—on the band saw (see Figure 3). Sand the edges smooth with a spindle sander (see Figure 4). A drum sander chucked into your drill press would also work.

Cut out the side lounging legs (pieces 4). The notch that fits into the front leg should

be part of the template. Lay out the three router-made, ¾"-wide openings on each leg. The two long parallel cuts are decorative. The short cut is actually a mortise made to accept the under brace (piece 5).

Next, machine the under brace, forming the tenons with a dado head installed in your table saw; use a miter gauge and a registration block clamped to your fence. Then, with a sharp chisel, carefully round over the tenons to match the router-made through mortises, testing the fit as you go.

Break the edges of the legs and back arm support with sandpaper, and then round over the top and bottom edges of the arms with a ¼" roundover bit (see Figure 5).

Now, assemble these pieces using Titebond III glue and screws. Counterbore the screws that are exposed, and then glue plugs into the counterbored holes, with the exception of those on the arms. Clamp a support to the back arm support to hold it in its appropriate position until the back slats are added.

The next step is to make the rear and front cross slats (pieces 6 and 7). Note that the rear slat has a 20° front edge. Mark their patterns, cut them to shape, and sand off the saw marks.

Attach the front cross slat with screws in counterbored holes, and plug the counterbored holes.

Now, locate the position of the rear cross slat by clamping two straight guide boards to the front edge of the back arm support. The boards should be long enough to rest on the under brace. Place the rear cross slat in its approximate position on top of the lounging legs, and slide it forward until it touches the guide boards. With the arms square to the front legs, and with the two angled faces of the back arm support and the rear cross slat flat to the guide boards, you have found the proper location for the cross slat. Later in the assembly, the back slats will occupy the space where the guide boards are during this step.

Attach the rear cross slat with screws in counterbored holes, and plug the counterbored holes.

Figure 3: *Shape the parts using a band saw with a ¼" blade. Some of the cloud lifts and curves require that tight corners be cut, as on this back slat.*

Figure 4: *To smooth edges, to remove saw marks, and even to help shape some of the curves, a spindle sander is a very handy tool to have on the job.*

Figure 5: *Use a trim router equipped with a ¼" roundover, bearing-guided bit to add emphasis to the chair's soft organic shapes.*

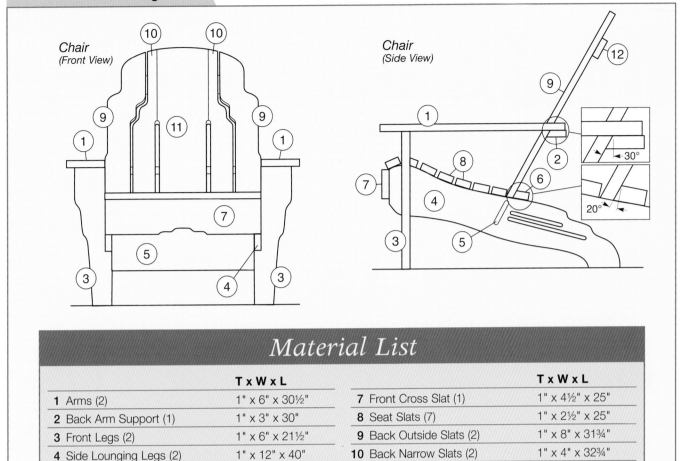

Chair
(Front View)

Chair
(Side View)

30°

20°

Material List

	T x W x L		T x W x L
1 Arms (2)	1" x 6" x 30½"	**7** Front Cross Slat (1)	1" x 4½" x 25"
2 Back Arm Support (1)	1" x 3" x 30"	**8** Seat Slats (7)	1" x 2½" x 25"
3 Front Legs (2)	1" x 6" x 21½"	**9** Back Outside Slats (2)	1" x 8" x 31¾"
4 Side Lounging Legs (2)	1" x 12" x 40"	**10** Back Narrow Slats (2)	1" x 4" x 32¾"
5 Under Brace (1)	1" x 6" x 25"	**11** Back Center Slat (1)	1" x 8" x 32¾"
6 Rear Cross Slat (1)	1" x 2½" x 25"	**12** Back Top Brace (1)	1" x 3¼" x 19"

Making the Remaining Slats

Make all seven seat slats (pieces 8). Attach all but the one closest to the rear cross slat. Set that piece aside for now. Secure the rest of the slats with screws in counterbored holes, and plug the counterbored holes.

While the back looks as if it is made from three pieces of stock, it is actually assembled from five separate pieces (pieces 9 through 11). Cut and shape the back slats as you did the earlier pieces, and glue the narrow and center back slats together, using Titebond III glue. Then, chuck a ¼" roundover bit in your router, and round over the appropriate edges of the back slats. Test fit the back slats. They should stand on top of the under brace, just as your guides did earlier. Make any necessary adjustments.

Next, make the back top brace (piece 12). Then, fasten the back slats to the back top brace and to the back arm support with screws in counterbored holes. Note that the screws driven

through the front face of the back slats should be drilled in the decorative pattern shown in the drawings on page 84. Plug the three counterbored holes on the face of the back top brace.

Now, attach the final seat slat as you did the others. It should touch the back slats.

Final Steps

Using a sharp chisel, chop shallow square mortises at each of the decoratively drilled screw holes and the exposed screw holes on the arms. Then, mix black (ebony) two-part epoxy, and fill the mortises you just formed. Allow the epoxy to cure.

Sand up through all the grits, taking your time, and then apply several coats of teak or other exterior oil finish. This will have to be refreshed from year to year.

Now, move this extraordinarily solid lawn chair outdoors, and accept its gracious invitation to have a seat.

Each square equals 1".

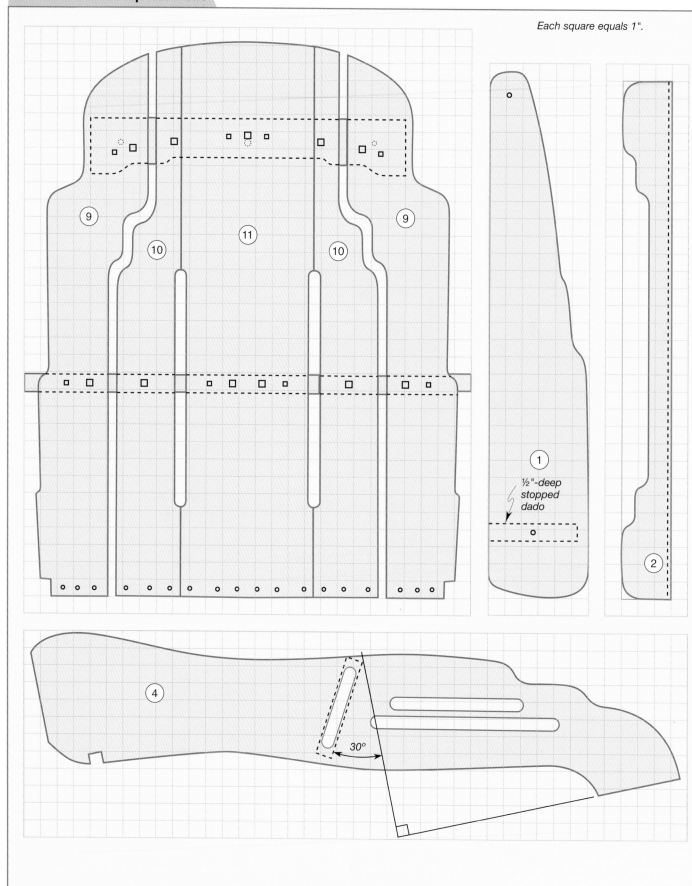

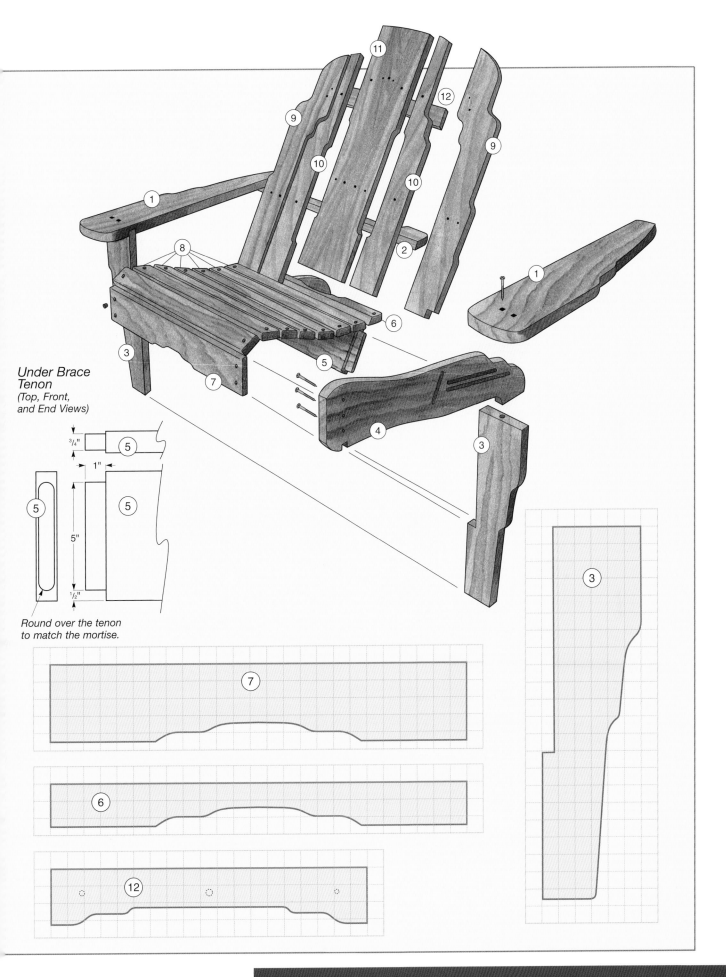

Under Brace
Tenon
*(Top, Front,
and End Views)*

³/₄"

1"

5"

¹/₂"

*Round over the tenon
to match the mortise.*

Portable Outdoor Chair

Nothing beats spending some leisure time in the great outdoors, whether that amounts to a quiet corner of the yard, the sidelines of a softball game, or the deep woods of the wilderness. Wherever you go, take these handy two-piece chairs along. Slide the parts together one way for use or another way for storage.

by Rick White

Whether you're sitting around a warm fire after a day on the boat, cooling your heels at camp after chasing upland game, or just leaning back and soaking up a couple of cold ones after you mow the lawn, it's nice to have a comfortable place to take a load off. These slide-together outdoor chairs are not a new idea; in fact, the inspiration for this updated white-oak version was rolled out more than 20 years ago in a summer issue of *Woodworker's Journal*. I spruced up the design a bit by making the chairs more compact when they are nested together for storage. I also added a few strategically placed double-screwed cleats, to eliminate the chance of racking.

White oak is an excellent choice for this project because of its strength and its durability against the elements. These chairs really don't eat up a lot of material—there are only about 12 board feet in each one, and you can probably raid your scrap bin for some of that. Other good lumber options are Spanish cedar, cypress, or redwood. You could also make them from poplar and finish them with primer and exterior paint.

Getting Started with a Pair of Templates

Rather than make just one chair, it's almost more efficient to make several at once and build them production-style. For the curved seat and backrest sides (pieces 1 and 2), start by making a couple of perfectly sized hardboard templates (see the pattern drawings for the seat and backrest sides on page 88). Trace around the templates to lay out a series of paired seat and backrest sides on your hardwood stock. Then, carefully cut these pieces to shape on the band saw, staying just a hair outside the layout lines (see Figure 1).

Next, use double-sided carpet tape to attach the templates to the stock for template routing, and add three small brads—just for insurance. With a ½" flush-trimming, bearing-guided router bit mounted in your router table, you're ready for final trimming (see Guide to Template Routing on page 90 for tips).

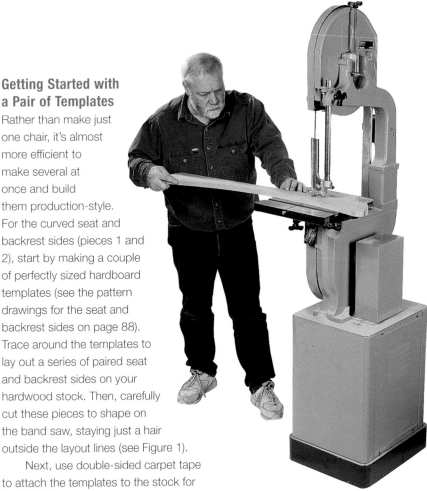

Figure 1: *With perfectly sized templates completed, transfer the shapes onto your stock for the seat and backrest sides. Then, band saw the pieces to shape, keeping just outside your pencil lines.*

Seat and Backrest Sides

Each square equals 1".

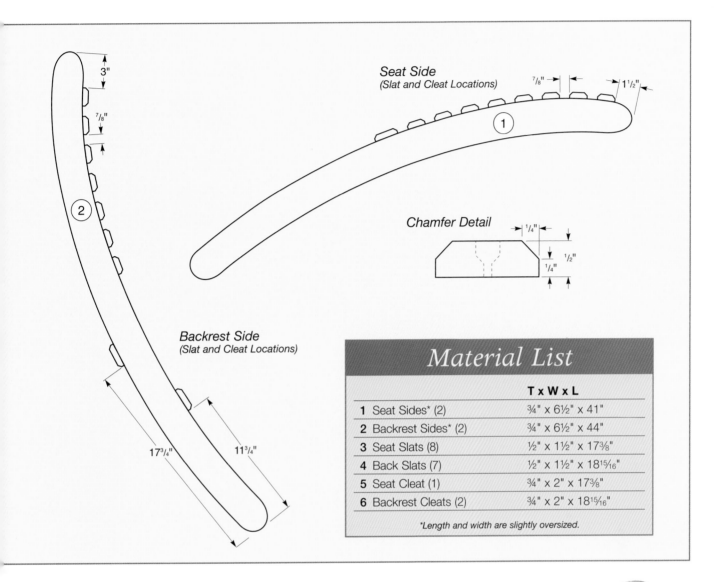

Seat Side
(Slat and Cleat Locations)

3"

⁷⁄₈"

1½"

①

②

⁷⁄₈"

Chamfer Detail

¼"

½"

¼"

Backrest Side
(Slat and Cleat Locations)

17¾"

11¾"

Material List		
	T x W x L	
1 Seat Sides* (2)	¾" x 6½" x 41"	
2 Backrest Sides* (2)	¾" x 6½" x 44"	
3 Seat Slats (8)	½" x 1½" x 17⅜"	
4 Back Slats (7)	½" x 1½" x 18¹⁵⁄₁₆"	
5 Seat Cleat (1)	¾" x 2" x 17⅜"	
6 Backrest Cleats (2)	¾" x 2" x 18¹⁵⁄₁₆"	

*Length and width are slightly oversized.

Be careful when you attempt to rout around the rounded ends of the parts. Trimming across the end grain can be problematic: If you leave too much waste material extending beyond the template to start with, the end grain can cause the bit to bite off more than it can chew and jerk the wood out of your hands or tear it up. The key is to band saw your stock so that you leave just the barest bit of waste material to be trimmed away by the flush-trimming cutter—particularly along the end grain; about ¹⁄₁₆" extra is perfect. Set your router for its highest speed, and use a ½"-shank cutter to minimize flexing.

Equally important, go slowly, and keep your hands clear of the bit! If the bit creates some burning on the ends, don't worry; it sands off pretty easily (see Figure 2). Go ahead and make all the shaped parts at one time.

Moving On to the Seat and Back Slats

The slats for the seat and back (pieces 3 and 4) have the same thickness and width, but they differ in length. Rip a sufficient quantity of slat stock, and then cut the pieces to their appropriate lengths. Again, if you are making more than one

Figure 2: *Cleaning up your edges on a spindle sander takes just a few minutes. One of the nice things about template routing is that it leaves just a few machining marks that are a snap to remove.*

Begin the template-routing sequence by using your template to trace the shape of the piece onto your hardwood stock. Step to the band saw and cut out the piece, staying just outside the line.

Attach the template to the stock with double-sided carpet tape. It's a good idea to drive a few small brads through the template, as well, to ensure that the template stays put during routing.

Template routing is a great way to ensure multiple pieces are identically shaped. It's also a great way to destroy parts and injure yourself if you are not careful. Here are four rules you should always follow:

1. Leave a bare 1/16" of stock to mill off.
2. Keep your hands well away from the cutter.
3. Attach templates securely to your stock.
4. Be keenly aware of the bit's rotation before you begin trimming.

One final caution: Template routing at each end of a piece (across the end grain) must be done slowly and with the utmost care. I suggest that you make a test run on scrap before you move to the real thing, so that you can get a feel for how the bit behaves when you move from long-grain to end-grain trimming.

chair, set up and cut the slats in groups. (It's a good idea to make a couple of extra slats, in case one or two split during assembly.) Drill and counterbore holes centered at each end of the slats (one setup works for both types of slats). You'll plug these holes later to hide the screws.

As long as you are ripping and drilling, go ahead and make the seat and backrest cleats (pieces 5 and 6) from 3/4" stock. The cleats are wider than the slats and have two screws in each end. They keep the backrest and seat assemblies from racking, although their main function is to lock the chair securely in each of its various seat positions. Cut them to size, and bore the screw holes (see Figure 3). Now, grab the slats and cleats, and move over to your router table. Chuck a chamfering bit in the router, and get busy easing the edges of the combined slats and cleats. Remember to ease only the edges that will face out when the chair is assembled.

Putting It All Together

If you have two drill drivers, get them ready. First, make a 7/8" x 7/8" x 20" spacer. Start attaching the seat and back slats, as shown in the drawings on pages 88–89, and use the spacer to locate each successive slat. Drill a pilot hole with the first drill, and then drive it home with the second. When you place the final seat slat, use the spacer again to locate the seat cleat. Make sure you square up the assembly before you drive these screws home. Simple as pie. When you've placed the last back slat, check the drawings once more to locate the backrest cleats.

Plug the screw holes with face-grain wood plugs and water-resistant glue. After the glue cures, give the chair assemblies a complete sanding. You are almost ready to sit back and make yourself comfortable.

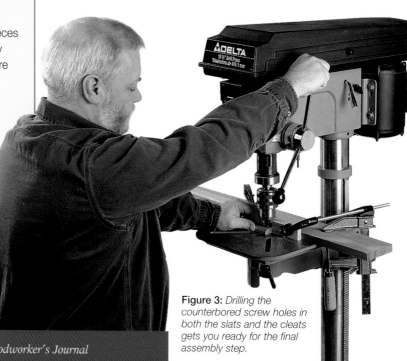

Figure 3: *Drilling the counterbored screw holes in both the slats and the cleats gets you ready for the final assembly step.*

Deadly Combo: Router Bits and End Grain

Using a flush-trimming, bearing-guided router bit to cut across end grain can lead to big trouble. Limiting the depth of the cut (and thus reducing the penetration of the cutter's blade) will greatly reduce your chance of splitting the wood.

For clarity, the template is not shown.

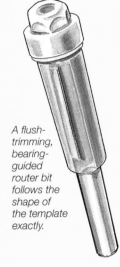

A flush-trimming, bearing-guided router bit follows the shape of the template exactly.

Great care must be used when routing around the ends of a template. The end grain is susceptible to fracturing, as shown in the illustration at far left, and rushing a cut can ruin your piece.

Finishing and Upkeep

There are several durable options for outdoor finishes, but I settled on an easily applied outdoor oil finish (see Figure 4). An exterior-grade polyurethane or spar varnish would also look great on these white-oak beauties—but eventually, it will scratch and chip with use, and sometimes the varnish will peel. An oil finish has other merits: It is easy to brush into nooks and crannies formed by the slats and cleats, it looks great, and most importantly, it is simple to touch up and renew. You will need to reapply the finish on any piece of outdoor furniture every couple of years to keep the wood looking good. Give these chairs a good cleaning and then a quick rubdown with a coat of oil, and they'll be ready for another season of outdoor adventures. Whether that includes a trip to the Boundary Waters Canoe Area or simply to the Outdoor Brew Area in your backyard is entirely up to you.

Figure 4: I used an outdoor oil finish on my chairs. Now, with a little bit of regular upkeep, they'll be ready for any outdoor adventure. You can be sure that I'll be putting them to good use after a long day of walleye fishing.

Canadian Ladder-Back Chair

This rustic ladder-back chair is similar to examples found in Quebec, Virginia, and other frontier areas in the early nineteenth century. The chair shown here was made mostly using hand tools. Give this a try if you're after a good challenge, or modify the construction so you can use your power tools instead.

by Stephen Shepherd

Frontier life in the early nineteenth century was an exercise in self-sufficiency. Hardscrabble settlers had to rely on their innate skills and a few basic hand tools to build and furnish their homesteads. Their furniture was simple and utilitarian, made to stand up to the rigors of daily life on the fringe of civilization.

This ladder-back side chair is typical of the furniture forms that evolved during that period, and it remains popular today. The chair shown here is patterned after an example found in Quebec. With its simple square tapered legs, turned or shaved rungs, and cut or bent back slats, it is easy to make with hand tools or power tools.

The seats of many Quebec chairs were strung with fine strips of rawhide or beaver skin in a traditional snowshoe pattern (see Weaving a Gut Seat: How to Do the Snowshoe Weave on page 98); but you can also use rush, Shaker cloth tape, or twisted sea wrack. It

takes me about 6 hours to build one of these chairs. Finishing it and stringing the seat takes another few hours.

Selecting the Wood

Early craftsmen made their chairs from any locally available woods. I've seen examples in chestnut, white oak, and ash, as well as in yellow birch, which was the wood of choice in Quebec.

Many of these chairs were made of plain-grained woods, such as poplar, spruce, and pine, and then painted, often with a brick-red color called Spanish brown. A few show evidence of original hand graining to imitate fancier woods.

Whichever wood you choose, try to select straight-grained stock for the front legs and rungs—it's stronger and easier to work with hand tools. The angled back legs and curved slats will be less apt to break under duress if the grain follows these curves.

Making the Legs and Rungs First

Look over the Material List on page 97. Then, make the back legs (pieces 1) first so you can use them to lay out the front legs, rungs, and slats (pieces 2 through 8). To make the chair more comfortable, the back legs tilt back 7° from the seat (see the drawings on page 97), so you'll have to band saw them from stock that is at least 3¼" wide. Taper the inside of the uprights, as shown in the drawings, to enhance the flare of the top of the chair. Notice that there are also four-sided tapers on the bottoms of the legs.

I dimensioned this chair with the seat 19" off the floor to suit my 6'-tall frame. If you prefer or need

Figure 1: *The rungs on the chair can be turned (above), or they can be shaped by hand with a drawknife and spokeshave (right). Either way, be sure to leave a slight belly on the tenons to create space for glue and to allow for slight variations in the angle.*

a lower seat, adjust the front leg height accordingly.

Since the legs are essentially square, you can clean them up easily with a hand plane and chamfer them with a hand plane or spokeshave. The only difficult area to plane is the inside angle of the back legs; you can use a spokeshave or scraper in this grain transition area.

Now, you can lay out the mortises on the back legs. Note that they are angled forward to match the curve of the back slats. Keep this angle in mind as you chop the mortises. If you're using a hollow-chisel mortiser or a drill press to remove the waste, you can establish this angle by placing wedges under the legs.

I turned the rungs for this chair, but you can also shape the rungs by hand, using your drawknife and spokeshave (see Figure 1). The best way to hold the blanks for hand shaping is to use a shaving horse, but a bench vise will do.

You can create a slight shoulder where the tenons begin, or you can let the curve blend into the tenons. I turn a slight belly on the tenons (see Figure 1) to create a little space for the glue and to allow for some variation in the angle. This method preserves the strength of the joint when the legs season fully

and shrink around the tenons. To keep the rungs from coming loose, make the legs from air-dried lumber (12% to 14% moisture content) and the rungs and back slats from kiln-dried wood (6% to 8% moisture content). You can dry the rungs yourself by heating them in a 250° oven for a couple of hours before creating the tenons. Chamfer the ends of the tenons to make assembly easier.

Note that the lower rear rung (piece 4) is shorter than the one above it. This splays out the tops of the back legs for more visual appeal and added comfort.

Making the Back Slats

This is a very simple chair, with only two back slats (pieces 7 and 8). Some early examples were strung with canvas or rawhide spanning the space between the slats. You could also add a middle slat for more support.

You can make the back slats either by sawing them from solid stock or by bending them. I sawed the slats for this chair with a bow saw, but you could use a band saw or shape them with an adze instead. If you decide to saw them, you will need a blank about 2½" thick. If possible, use blanks with grain that follows the curved profile of the back slats.

If you want to steam bend the slats, cut the blanks to the rough size, steam them until they are pliable, and then clamp them over a form. For steaming, I place a section of stove pipe in a pot of water on the stove, bring the water to boil, and suspend the slats inside the pipe on a piece of wire threaded through a tiny hole in one end. After 15 to 20 minutes, I place them in a three-stick jig. After the bent pieces have dried, they can be cleaned up with planes and spokeshaves.

If you're using green wood, you can bend the back slats without steaming. Just split the wood into blanks of uniform thickness, plane them smooth, and bend them in the three-stick jig.

Whichever method you use to form the curves, be sure the ends are of uniform thickness so they will fit nicely into the mortises in the back legs. Rough cut the ends to fit the mortises, but don't cut these pieces to final length yet; those dimensions will depend on how the chair goes together.

Drilling the Rung Sockets

Once you've cut all the parts to their final shape, bore the round mortises, or sockets, for the tenons. Though I own a compound drill press that easily drills holes at complex angles, I prefer to drill these holes by hand, using a sharp Jennings-pattern twist auger and a beechwood brace.

I also use a hand-forged bit extension to get a good visual line on the angle as I'm drilling. You can use a spade bit with an extension for this step, but one of the subtleties of using an auger with a lead screw is that you can determine the exact depth of the mortise by counting the number of revolutions of the brace (see Figure 2).

The lower rungs of the chair are staggered so their sockets miss each other in the legs; but the top rungs are only partially offset, so they overlap when assembled, as shown in the chair drawings on page 97. The higher side rungs make the seat more comfortable.

The overlapping tenons add mechanical strength to the top rung joints, but this overlapping means you'll have to dry fit the front and back subassemblies before drilling the sockets for the top side rungs. Using this approach, you'll be drilling partway into the top rung tenons.

Later, when you're ready for the glue, be sure to orient the grain of the top rungs with the quarter-sawn grain perpendicular to the quarter-sawn grain of the legs to get the most benefit from the shrinkage effect, as shown in the grain orientation drawing on page 97.

Figure 3: *To find the correct drilling angle for the rung sockets, arrange the chair parts on the floor, and use a bevel gauge to sight the angle.*

Note that the sockets for the front rungs are drilled at 90° to the front legs in both directions, while the back rung sockets are angled upward slightly to accommodate the splay of the back. To establish this angle, I arrange the back legs and rungs on the floor and use a bevel gauge to eyeball the angle (see Figure 3). Don't worry too much about absolute precision; you can compensate somewhat during final assembly.

Drilling the sockets for the side rungs is a little more complicated because the front leg assembly is wider than the back, and the back leg assembly is narrower at the bottom than at the top. To determine the angles for the side rung sockets, I place the front leg assembly on the floor and raise the back leg assembly to its approximate position; then, I use my long bit extension to sight the correct angles as I drill (see Figure 2). You could be more scientific about it by figuring out the exact angles from the drawings and making angled plywood guides for zeroing in your drill bit.

Fitting the Slats

The final construction step is to fit the curved back slats into the back leg mortises. Begin by dry fitting the back assembly to establish the length of the slats, and then cut the slats to final shape and size. The top slat is longer due to the taper of the legs and the splay created by the back rungs.

Dry fit the two subassemblies again before glue-up. Make sure that all the sockets and mortises are the correct depth and angle and that the chair sits squarely on all four legs. You can make minor final adjustments during glue-up.

Hot hide glue is my first choice for all furniture, but liquid hide glue, which is more convenient and more readily available, is also good. The biggest advantage of hide glue is that it is reversible, should you ever need to disassemble the chair in the future. If you aren't concerned about downstream repairs, then use regular yellow glue.

Glue up the front and back leg assemblies first, carefully orienting the front and back upper rungs so their tenons are lined up in the sockets correctly (see the overlapping tenons detail drawing on page 96). Now, glue the four side rungs in place to bring the

Figure 2: *Use a bit extension to get a good visual line on the angle as you drill the rung socket. One of the subtleties of using an auger with a lead screw is that you can determine the depth of the mortise by counting the number of revolutions of the brace.*

Figure 4: *Hot hide glue is the best choice for this project (and for all furniture) because it's reversible.*

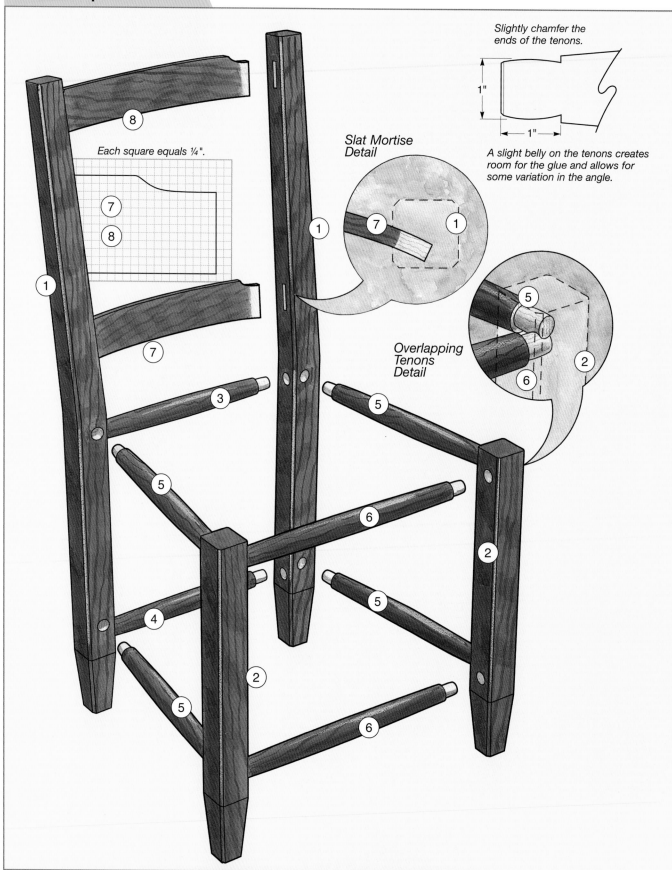

Each square equals ¼".

Slat Mortise Detail

Slightly chamfer the ends of the tenons.

1"

1"

A slight belly on the tenons creates room for the glue and allows for some variation in the angle.

Overlapping Tenons Detail

Chair
(Back View)

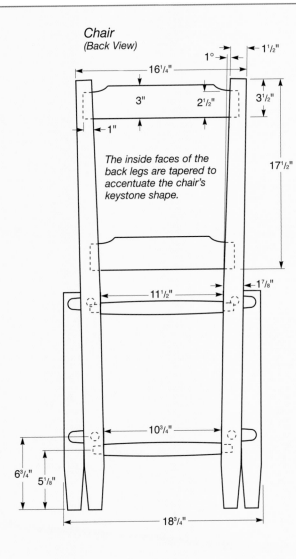

The inside faces of the back legs are tapered to accentuate the chair's keystone shape.

Material List

		T x W x L
1	Back Legs (2)	1⅞" x 3¼" x 39⅝"
2	Front Legs (2)	1⅞" x 1⅞" x 20"
3	Upper Rear Rung (1)	1⅜" Dia. x 13½"
4	Lower Rear Rung (1)	1⅜" Dia. x 12¾"
5	Side Rungs (4)	1⅜" Dia. x 14¾"
6	Front Rungs (2)	1⅜" Dia. x 17"
7	Bottom Slat* (1)	½" x 3" x 15¾"
8	Top Slat* (1)	½" x 3" x 15¾"
9	Rawhide Bend (1)	¼" x 36'

* Final sizing done during dry assembly.

NOTE: This chair was designed with a 19" seat height, to suit a 6'-tall sitter. Shorter people may choose to lower the seat (no more than 3") for their own comfort.

To get maximum benefit from the shrinkage effect, orient the grain of the top rungs as shown below.

Grain Orientation

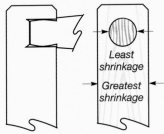

Least shrinkage

Greatest shrinkage

Chair
(Side View)

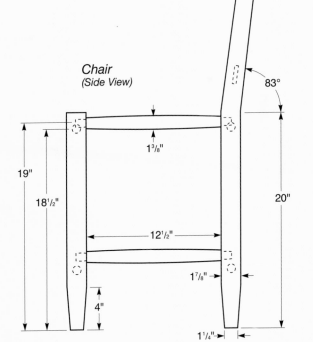

83°

NOTE: Make the slats a little oversize, and cut them to final size during a dry assembly of the back legs and rungs.

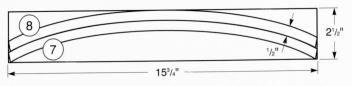

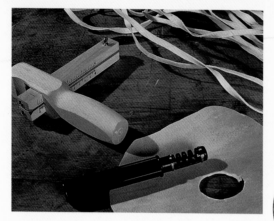

Begin by cutting a circle of cowhide with your scissors or with a lace-making tool (Tandy Leather, Item #3784-00). Place the tool in a hole in the center of your circle, start the cut, and pull on the end of the strip. The rawhide spins around the cutter as you pull the strip through the cutter.

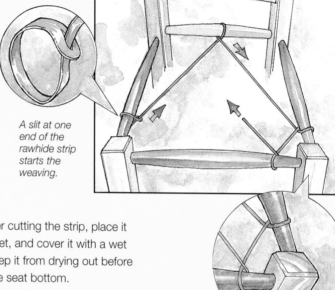

A slit at one end of the rawhide strip starts the weaving.

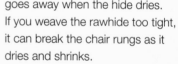

Many different materials have been used for weaving rustic chair seats, but in Quebec, where this chair originated, gut (usually beaver rawhide) was the material of choice. Patterned after the weave of traditional snowshoes, the gut seat is strong, attractive, and easy to make.

The best material I've found for gut seats is untanned cow rawhide "bends" (available from Tandy Leather, 800-433-3201, *www.tandyleather.com*, Item #9097-01). The only things you need to make one of these durable seats are a circle of rawhide, a pair of heavy scissors, a bucket of water, and a lace or strap cutter.

1. Cutting the Gut

To make this seat, you'll need a uniform strip of rawhide ¼" wide x 36' long. Rawhide is tough, so it's important to soak it in water until it is soft and pliable before trying to cut it. Soak it about 6 hours—not much longer, though, or it will become difficult to handle.

Begin by cutting a 14" circle of cowhide with your scissors. For strips over ⁵⁄₁₆" wide, you'll need to use scissors or a strap cutter (Tandy Leather, Item #3080-00), which is much like a cutting-type marking gauge. After cutting the strip, place it into a bucket, and cover it with a wet towel to keep it from drying out before weaving the seat bottom.

If you run out of rawhide strip, you can add to your first strip with the simple interlocking joint shown in the detail drawing at far right, bottom.

2. Weaving the Diagonals

This weaving pattern includes diagonal and side-to-side lacing. Begin by weaving the diagonals. Cut a slit in the end of the rawhide strip, and pull it around the side rung near the left front leg. Thread the entire strip through the slit, and pull it tight. Wrap the strip around the center of the back rung and back over itself, and then forward to the right rung, as shown in the drawing above. Continue this pattern, with the strips about 1½" apart, until you've covered the seat opening, ending up in the back left corner.

The lacing should be tight enough not to sag but not too tight; there will be some flex in the wet rawhide, but that goes away when the hide dries. If you weave the rawhide too tight, it can break the chair rungs as it dries and shrinks.

3. Weaving the Horizontal

To create the six-point star pattern, you weave the gut from side to side, over and under the diagonal strips, as shown in the drawing at right. The side-to-side weaving begins at the back of the left side rung with a double loop. After each course of weaving, loop the strip around the diagonal points of attachment, and then continue back to the other side, ending at the front of the left side rung where you began the diagonal weave. Secure the end with a knot.

4. Finishing Up

When you've finished the weaving, allow the rawhide to dry completely and tighten up. Lightly sand the dry rawhide to remove the surface fuzz. You can also do this with a sootless flame from a propane torch, but be careful to keep the flame moving. I like to finish my gut seats with a coat of marine spar varnish. This makes the rawhide translucent and affords a measure of protection for the leather when cleaning it.

Figure 5: *A rope-and-stick tourniquet (or a band clamp) makes short work of clamping the glued-up chair.*

chair together (see Figure 4 on page 95). Brush a generous coating of glue on all the joints, and then clamp the chair together using a rope-and-stick tourniquet (see Figure 5) or a band clamp.

After the chair has been clamped up, place it on a flat surface to make sure that it dries flat and square. I use a flat cast-iron table for this, but a flat workbench is fine. If the chair has a stubborn little twist in the structure, you can clamp the legs to the table to straighten it out.

Once the glue has set for a while and the wood has absorbed some of the moisture from the hide glue, wipe off any excess glue, and then tighten the clamps again.

When the glue has dried, you have the option of installing hardwood pegs to lock the tenons in place and to add a decorative effect. If you don't want the pegs to show, drill the peg holes from the inside or back and don't drill all the way through. You can use regular dowels for the pegs, or you can whittle them instead.

Now, all that's left to do is to add the rawhide (piece 9) to make the seat, as explained at left.

The transition from diagonal to horizontal weaving begins at the back of the left side rung with a double loop.

NOTE: *The snowshoe weave pattern creates an even number of wraps (8 in this case) on the back rung, balanced by an odd number (7) on the front rung. Likewise, there are 4 wraps on the right rung, and 5 on the left.*

The diagonal weave is shown in gold, while the horizontal weave is shown in blue.

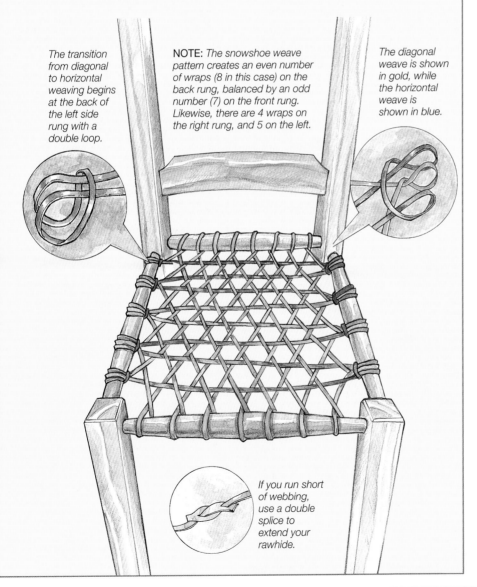

If you run short of webbing, use a double splice to extend your rawhide.

Cherry Dining Chair

Whether you set your sights on building eight for a dining room or just want one for a bedroom, try your hand at chair making. Chances are, you'll find it a whole lot easier than you've been led to believe. Walk step-by-step through the process by building this handsome cherry dining chair.

by Chris Inman

Chair making has an undeserved reputation for difficulty. While you do have to consider the special stresses that chairs are subject to, there are plenty of solutions already figured out by those who have gone before us. Furthermore, if you have a chair plan in hand, the most difficult part is behind you.

If you're concerned about the upholstered seats on this chair, put your mind at ease. Not only is this an uncomplicated chair to cover, but step-by-step instructions are provided in Three-Step Upholstery on page 104 to help you work through this part of the project. There are also many good books on the subject, which you may find helpful to study. And finally, if you have an itch to build the chair but don't want to tackle the upholstery, there are craftspeople everywhere who do this for a living and who would gladly cap off your fine work with their own.

One technique you might not have tried before that's used in constructing this chair is bent lamination. This is the process of face gluing several thin boards together while they're pressed in a form. When the glue dries, the assembly retains the shape of the form. It's about the easiest way to bend wood, and learning the technique will open up new doors for your woodworking designs.

The Material List on page 103 itemizes the supplies you'll need for one chair. If you plan to build a set of six or eight chairs, be sure to multiply your supply list by that number, and remember to multiply your material fudge factor by the number of chairs you plan on building. To build one chair, you'll need a total of 6 board feet of 1¾"-thick lumber for the legs and 6 board feet of ¾"-thick stock for the rest. Buy about 30% more stock than you need, to allow for wood defects and those inevitable mistakes that require making a new workpiece.

Starting with the Legs

Once you have the legs cut to shape and the mortises routed in, your chair will be well on its way. Begin working toward that goal by making a ¼"-thick plywood template for the rear legs (pieces 1). To make the template, start by using a

Figure 1: *Cut out a slightly oversize rear leg on a band saw, and then secure your plywood template to the stock with double-sided tape. Next, rout the leg to its finished size with a piloted flush-cutting bit.*

Figure 2: *To make the mortises, first remove the bulk of the waste by drilling several holes with a ⅜" bit. Then, connect the holes, square the ends, and smooth the mortise walls with sharp chisels.*

photocopier to enlarge the pair of patterns for the rear leg on page 107. Then, tape the two sections together, and glue them to a piece of ¼" plywood. Next, staying about ¹⁄₁₆" outside the pattern, cut the plywood to shape with a band saw. Now, make a very accurate template by filing and sanding the plywood right to the pattern line.

The next step is to make the mortise layout openings in the template. Remove most of the waste at the mortise

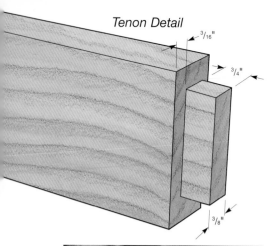

Tenon Detail

3/16"

3/4"

3/8"

Figure 3: *Although the rail and stretcher sizes vary, the basic tenon-cutting operation remains the same. Cut the cheeks on a table saw, remove the edge waste with a handsaw, and then pare the shoulders with a chisel. Paring the shoulders until they're flush all around ensures a perfect fit.*

positions shown on the pattern by drilling through the plywood, and then use a chisel, a file, and sandpaper to refine these openings.

With the rear leg template completed, prepare your leg stock for all four legs. First, plane your lumber to a thickness of 1⅝", and then rip enough wood for the two front legs (pieces 2). On the rest of the plank, trace the shape of the template twice for the rear legs. Now, band saw around the rear legs, cutting about 1/16" away from the line as you did when making the template. You'll remove the excess shortly with a router.

The effort you spent making the plywood template will now pay off by helping rout the rear legs to final shape. Secure the template to the inside face of one of the rear legs with long strips of double-sided tape, making sure that the cherry evenly overhangs the plywood all the way around. Press the template securely in place to ensure that it won't slip out of position during routing. Next, set up your router table with a laminate-trimming bit that has a cutting length of 2". Rout the first leg by running the

template against the bit's bearing, and then repeat the procedure for the second leg (see Figure 1 on page 101). Although the photo doesn't show it, it's a good idea to start these template cuts with the workpiece pressed against a starter pin installed in your router table.

With the legs routed to their final shape, clamp the legs together, and use a scraper and sander to smooth them until they match perfectly.

The four legs have reached their basic form, so now it's time to cut the mortises. Lay out the mortises on the legs using your rear leg template and the front leg pattern drawing on page 107. Note that the leg mortises must mirror each other—not be exact copies. Therefore, mark their positions carefully, and label the legs *right* and *left* for positioning.

Next, chuck a ⅜" bit in your drill press, and bore out most of the waste in each mortise to a depth of ¾" (see Figure 2 on page 101), with the exception of the crest rail mortises, which should be drilled all the way through. Because of the angle on

the lower part of the rear legs, use a handheld drill for clearing out the mortises for the side stretchers. Once the mortise waste has been drilled out, use a chisel to square the ends and smooth the side walls to finish the job.

Cutting the Tenons

With the legs ready for assembly, you now need to make the seat rails (pieces 3), stretchers (pieces 4 and 5), back support rail (piece 6), and crest rail (piece 7). Cut ¾"-thick lumber for the rails and stretchers to the dimensions given in the Material List (note that these lengths include the tenons).

Once the pieces have been cut to size, set aside the crest rail for a moment, and cut the tenons on the other chair parts. Install a ¾" dado blade in your table saw and raise it 3/16". Clamp a clearance block to the fence to keep the operation safe, and set the fence so the block is in line with the blade. It's wise to make a few test passes so you're sure that the cuts are square and that the tenons fit the

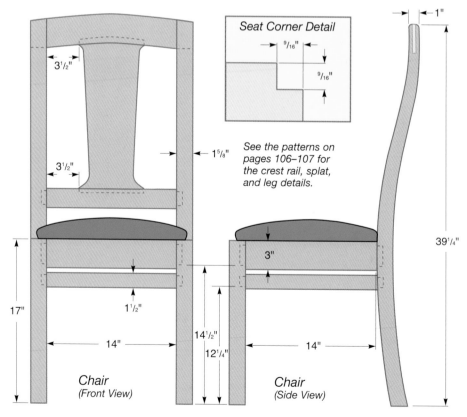

Seat Corner Detail

9/16"

9/16"

See the patterns on pages 106–107 for the crest rail, splat, and leg details.

3½"

3½"

1⅝"

1"

17"

14"

1½"

14½"

12¼"

3"

14"

39¼"

Chair
(Front View)

Chair
(Side View)

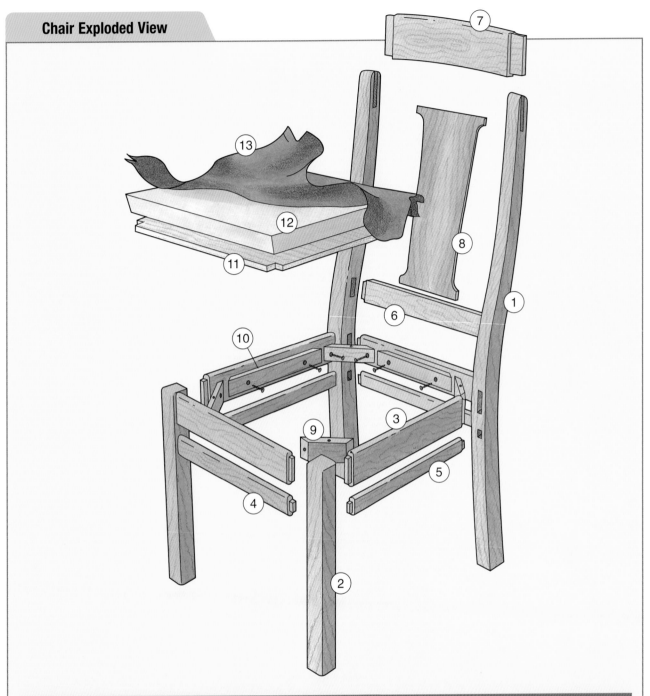

Material List

		T x W x L			T x W x L
1	Rear Legs (2)	1⅝" x 1⅝" x 40"	**8**	Splat (1)	⁵⁄₁₆" x 7" x 15½"
2	Front Legs (2)	1⅝" x 1⅝" x 17"	**9**	Corner Blocks (4)	¾" x 1½" x 4"
3	Seat Rails (4)	¾" x 3" x 15½"	**10**	Seat Support Strips (4)	¾" x 1½" x 11"
4	Stretchers (2)	¾" x 1½" x 15½"	**11**	Seat (1)	⅜" x 15¼" x 15¼"
5	Side Stretchers (2)	¾" x 1½" x 16"	**12**	Foam Cushion (1)	2" x 17" x 17"
6	Back Support Rail (1)	¾" x 2" x 15½"	**13**	Fabric (1)	24" x 24"
7	Crest Rail (1)	¾" x 4" x 15½"			

Three-Step Upholstery

Step 1: *Cut your 2"-thick high-density foam on a band saw with the table tilted at 30°. Cut the foam so its smaller face equals the size of the plywood seat.*

Step 2: *Pull the side flaps around the seat first, continuously shooting in staples along the fabric. To keep the padding smooth, be sure to adjust the tension in the fabric as you go.*

Step 3: *Pull the corner flaps toward the center of the seat, and staple them. Then, pull the front and back flaps around, while making sure to get a crisp crease in each corner.*

Cutting the fabric properly makes the upholstering steps go a lot easier. Trim the fabric to a 24" x 24" square, and then remove the corner waste to the dimensions shown at right. Next, make the corner flap cuts. The fabric edges with the flaps should be used on the front and back edges of the seat.

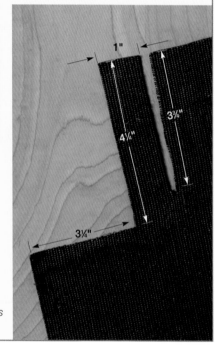

Figure 4: *Cut the tenon on the angled end of each side stretcher by hand.*

1½"   1"

Slightly angled shoulder

mortises. Now, cut tenons on both ends of each piece, except for the side stretchers, which have machine-cut tenons on the front end only.

To cut the crest rail tenons, reset the fence 1¾" from the dado blade, and make several passes to remove the cheek waste. These tenons will reach through the open-ended mortises on the tops of the rear legs.

The tenons aren't done until the edge shoulders are cut with a handsaw and trimmed with a sharp chisel. Carefully cut each shoulder a little fat,

and use a chisel to shave the shoulders flush (see Figure 3 on page 102). On the crest rail, cut the bottom edge only.

Put together the legs and seat rail for each side of the chair, and while these pieces are assembled, position the side stretchers on the assemblies. Mark the angled rear shoulder on each stretcher, and lay out the ⅜"-thick tenons. Then, use a handsaw and chisel to cut the tenons (see Figure 4).

The finished crest rail has a mild curve on its top and bottom edges, as shown in the pattern on page 107. Enlarge the pattern on a photocopier, cut it out, and then trace it onto your crest rail stock. Use a band saw to cut the crest rail to shape, and then sand the edges smooth.

The crest rail and back support rail house the back splat (piece 8) in 5/16"-wide x ½"-deep grooves. These grooves are easily routed with a ¼" slot cutter by making two passes that are slightly offset from each other. Draw lines on the rails to indicate the length and width of the grooves (see the chair drawings on page 102) on the appropriate edge of each piece. Make the first pass so the bit cuts along the top of the 5/16" groove layout, and then lower the cutter to widen the slot to the full 5/16" area. Square the slot ends with a ¼" chisel.

Right now, the chair parts are all quite sharp, but the completed chair will feel more comfortable if the edges are rounded. To accomplish this, install a ⅜"-radius roundover bit in your router table, and rout the edges of all the stretchers and rails, as well as the front corner of each front leg. On the grooved edges of the crest rail and lower back support, cut a slight chamfer with a hand plane. Now, thoroughly sand all the chair pieces to 120 grit.

Assembling the Chair

Most of your chair parts are made and ready for assembly now. The one piece you've completed but don't want to assemble is the crest rail, which you'll add after the splat is installed. Collect all your chair pieces, and set your glue bottle nearby. The best procedure for assembling the chair is to first glue up each side so you have a right and left subassembly. Then, after the glue has dried, join the two sides with the front and back rails, stretchers, and lower back support. Building the chair in sections helps make the assembly easier to clamp. Be sure to shear away any glue squeeze-out with a chisel once it gets rubbery.

As we all know, chairs are subject to extraordinary stress, and one way of reinforcing them is to add corner blocks (pieces 9) to each leg-and-seat-rail joint. Cut four pieces of ¾" stock to size, and then tilt your table saw blade 45° to miter the ends of each block. Before installing the blocks, drill a counterbored pilot hole through the bottom edge of each piece so that later you'll have a way to screw the seat to the chair. Now, drill countersunk pilot holes into the mitered ends of the corner blocks, and screw them to the inside corners of the seat structure, leaving a ½" reveal (see Figure 5).

It's a good idea to install the seat support strips (pieces 10) at this time, as well. Rip enough stock to make the four strips, and then miter them to length to fit between the corner blocks on the inside of the seat rails. Drill countersunk pilot holes in the strips, and screw them ½" from the top edges of the rails.

Making the Splat

The splat looks like solid wood that has been bent in a steaming process. But actually, it's made up of three thin layers that are laminated together. This method of curving wood is called bent lamination. The splat is 7" wide, but most band saws can only resaw wood up to 6"; so it's best to work with narrower stock now and then join it after the bending process to get the required width. Begin by resawing a 1¾"-thick x 3¾"-wide plank into six 5/32"-thick pieces. Choose wood that highlights the chair with a special grain pattern or coloring, like the sapwood

Figure 5: *Corner blocks ease excessive stress on a chair and serve as a base for securing the seat.*

Counterbore and pilot hole

45°
¾"
4"

streak in this chair (see Figure 6). As the pieces are cut, number them for easy ordering later.

Now, separate the pieces into two piles. Place pieces 1, 3, and 5 in one pile, and set the even-numbered pieces in the second pile. Later, when you glue the two halves of the splat together, piece 1 will mate with piece 2 and so on, creating a book-matched joint for the splat.

The laminations are cut, but you need to smooth the surfaces so they bond well with adhesive. The best gluing surface is one that's planed, either with a hand plane or with a planer and special backup board. The backup board supports the relatively weak laminations and enables the machining of such thin material. Cut a ¾"-thick piece of plywood to about 8" x 21", and use double-sided tape to secure the number 1 and number 2 laminations to the panel. Be sure to use two or three strips of tape under each lamination; otherwise, the pressing action of the bed rollers will cause an irregular planing pattern. Plane both sides of the first

pieces to just under ⅛" in thickness, and follow with the remaining two pairs of laminations. The combined thickness of each separate stack of numbered pieces should equal 5/16".

Now, it's time to make a particleboard lamination form following the curve shown in the drawings; it matches the curve atop the crest rail. Cut and rout the stack of form pieces, and then bond them together with yellow glue. Next, mix urea-formaldehyde glue according to the manufacturer's directions, and spread this glue on one stack of cherry laminations. Set the laminations in the form, add the backer strips, and pull the strips around and against the form with clamps (see Figure 7 on page 106). Allow the lamination to dry overnight, and then work on the other stack.

Once both halves of the splat have been removed from the form, clean up the glue, and then joint the mating edges. Join the two halves of the splat with yellow glue and bar clamps.

The front profile of the splat is shown in the pattern on page 106. Enlarge the pattern, and then trace it onto the splat stock. Then, cut the splat to shape with a band saw. Check the fit of the splat in the back support and crest rail grooves, and make any necessary adjustments. Sand the splat thoroughly once you're satisfied with the fit, and then install the splat in the back support groove. Finally, glue the crest rail to the rear legs. Leave the splat unglued to allow for seasonal movement.

With the chair assembly completed, there's a little edge routing to do before applying the finish. First, trim the tops of the rear legs with a handsaw so they continue the curve established by the crest rail, and trim the front legs so they're flush with the seat rails. Next, use your router and a ⅜" roundover bit to ease the top edges of the rear legs and the top front edges of the front legs.

Figure 6: *Book-matching sapwood in the splat makes for an interesting and unique highlight on the chair.*

Figure 7: *To even the clamping pressure on the thin laminations, use backer strips of plastic laminate and bending plywood or untempered hardboard.*

Finishing Up

A hand-rubbed penetrating oil is unmatched as a finish for cherry. Rub in four coats of the oil, and top it off with a coat of paste wax to create a beautiful, rich patina. When the finishing is done, turn your attention to choosing a fabric for the seat and learning something about upholstery.

The first step toward upholstering the chair is to cut out the plywood seat (piece 11). Once the fit is good, notch the corners (see the detail drawing of the seat corner on page 102), and rout the top edges with a ¼" roundover bit. Relieving the plywood edges will prevent the wood from tearing the fabric and make for a more comfortable seat. Now, visit your local do-it-yourself upholstery shop to select some heavy-duty 2"-thick foam (piece 12) and a durable fabric (piece 13) for the cushion.

The steps for covering a simple chair seat are described on page104. Cover the seat, and then secure the cushion to the chair by driving a screw up through each corner block and into the plywood seat.

A set of chairs like this could well be a crowning ensemble for any dining room, or the chair alone could make an ideal accent for a bedroom or study. You'll probably find that once you've made one chair, the process for replicating it will go much faster when building more. Whether you build one or more chairs, it's encouraging to learn that chair making is just another branch of woodworking, and it's not nearly as difficult as you might have believed.

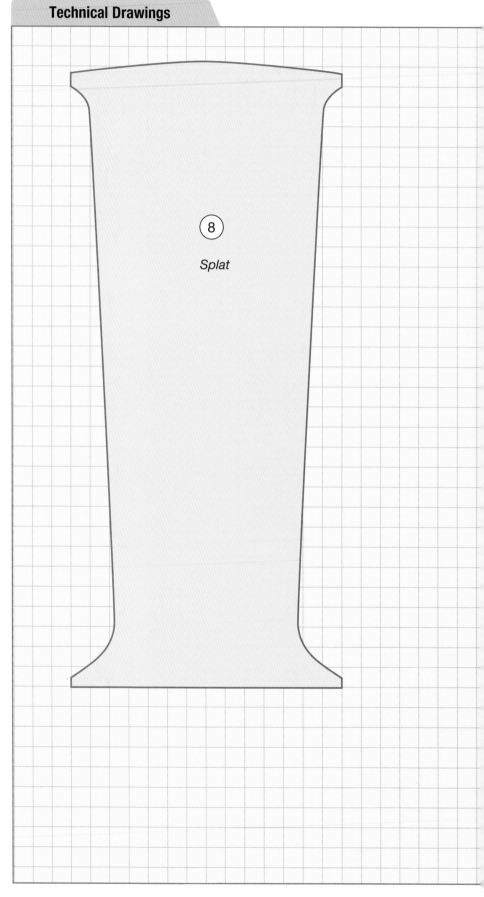

Technical Drawings

⑧

Splat

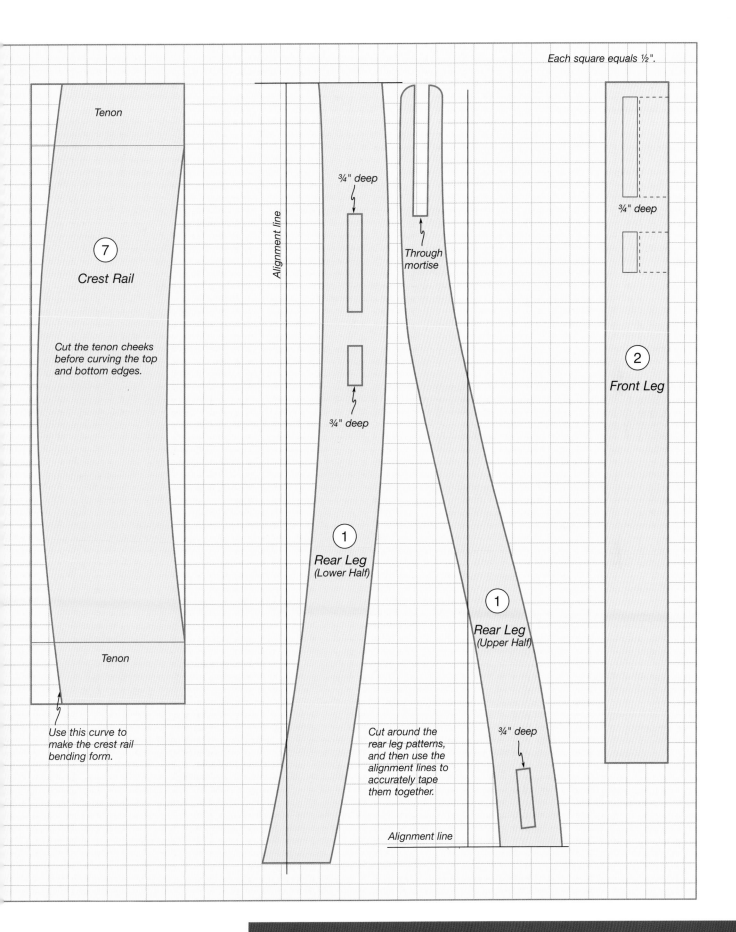

Each square equals ½".

Tenon

⑦

Crest Rail

Cut the tenon cheeks before curving the top and bottom edges.

Tenon

Use this curve to make the crest rail bending form.

Alignment line

¾" deep

¾" deep

Through mortise

①

Rear Leg (Lower Half)

①

Rear Leg (Upper Half)

¾" deep

Cut around the rear leg patterns, and then use the alignment lines to accurately tape them together.

Alignment line

¾" deep

②

Front Leg

Beds

by Rick White

Space-Saving Fold-Down Bed

A fold-down bed is already a great space saver, but now, with this drop-leaf desk addition, you get even more efficiency. Plus, you get to build two projects in one. This bed is the perfect solution for that small guest bedroom that doubles as a sewing room or the bedroom that your college student uses for the summer months.

Looking at a typical fold-down bed system can make the task of building one of these beds seem pretty daunting. There are springs and cables everywhere, adjustments and counter-adjustments, levers and wires, and from every angle, the contraption just looks confusing and difficult to assemble. It's little wonder that some clever people came up with a better alternative. The fold-down bed hardware that I discovered for this project has been in use in the hotel industry for years, but it was introduced only recently to the general public. The heart of the system is a piston, which controls the swing speed of the bed as it's opened or closed. The piston is fully enclosed, simple to install, and maintenance free.

Another problem with most fold-down beds is that, while they save space in a room, they're not very useful when they're not being slept in. That was the design challenge for this project. I think having a drop-leaf desk to use when you don't have overnight company is the perfect solution!

Without a doubt, this is a large plywood project, and there are several steps when a second set of hands will be helpful. In addition to enlisting some helpers, make sure the project will fit through the door of your workshop when it's done. Thinking ahead on both of these counts will save you pounds' worth of frustration.

Figure 1: *To apply pressure-sensitive edge banding, just peel back the protective paper and press the banding onto the plywood with a firm roller. You can also buy iron-on edge tape that works just as well.*

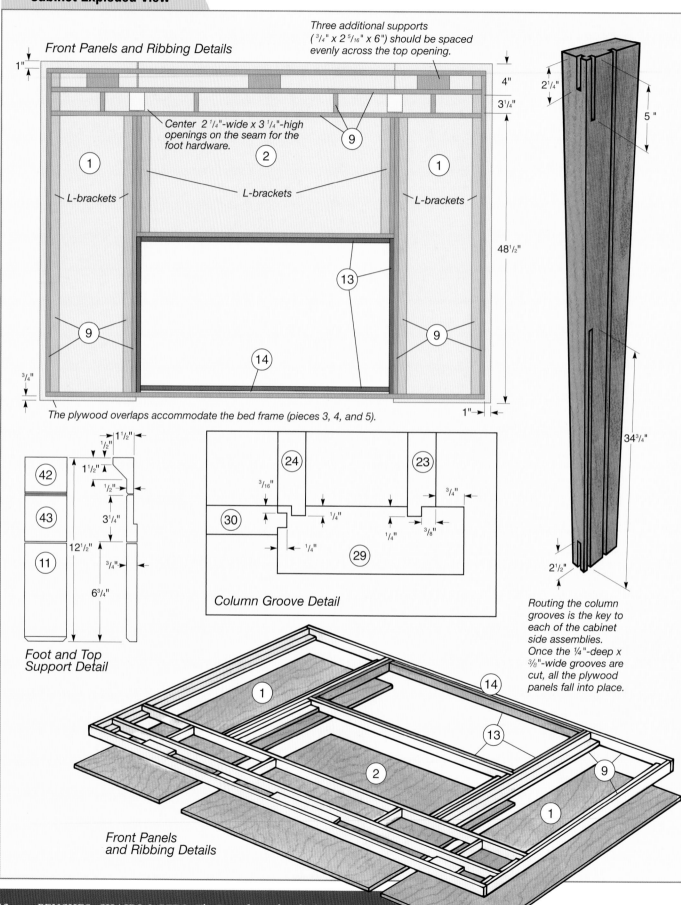

Front Panels and Ribbing Details

1"

Three additional supports
($^3/_4$" x 2 $^5/_{16}$" x 6") should be spaced
evenly across the top opening.

4"

3$^1/_4$"

Center 2 $^1/_4$"-wide x 3 $^1/_4$"-high
openings on the seam for the
foot hardware.

9

1   2   1

L-brackets   L-brackets   L-brackets

13

48$^1/_2$"

9   9

14

$^3/_4$"

The plywood overlaps accommodate the bed frame (pieces 3, 4, and 5).

1"

2$^1/_4$"

5 "

34$^3/_4$"

2$^1/_2$"

*Routing the column
grooves is the key to
each of the cabinet
side assemblies.
Once the ¼"-deep x
³⁄₈"-wide grooves are
cut, all the plywood
panels fall into place.*

1$^1/_2$"
$^1/_2$"
1$^1/_2$"
$^1/_2$"
3$^1/_4$"
12$^1/_2$"
$^3/_4$"
6$^3/_4$"

42
43
11

**Foot and Top
Support Detail**

24   23

30

$^3/_{16}$" $^1/_4$" $^3/_4$"

$^1/_4$" $^3/_8$"

29

$^1/_4$"

Column Groove Detail

1

14

13

2

9

1

**Front Panels
and Ribbing Details**

Material List

		T x W x L
1	Front Outside Panels (2)	¾" x 16¼" x 55¾"
2	Front Middle Panel (1)	¾" x 44½" x 28½"
3	Bed Frame Ends (2)	¾" x 6" x 54"
4	Bed Frame Side (1)	¾" x 6" x 76½"
5	Bed Frame Side (1)	¾" x 8" x 76½"
6	Plywood Banding (1)	13/16" x 50'
7	Screws	#8-2" (Bag of 100)
8	Plugs	⅜" Face Grain
9	Ribbing (9)	¾" x 1½" x 96"
10	Screws	#8-1¼" (Bag of 100)
11	Feet (2)	¾" x 3" x 6¾"
12	Fold-Down Bed Hardware (1)	
13	Desk Framing (1)	¾" x 2¼" x 142"
14	Filler Strip (1)	½" x 2¼" x 44½"
15	Desk (1)	¾" x 43" x 20¾"
16	Desk Supports (2)	¾" x 6" x 20"

(Material List continued on page 114.)

Plywood Cutting Guide

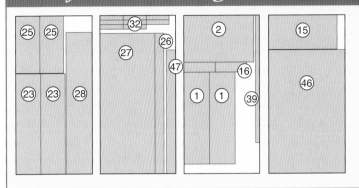

Building the Bed Box

Due to the special needs of the hardware installation, the bed box must be built first, and then the cabinet can be built around it. This seems awkward, but if you don't follow this sequence, you'll end up with two boxes that don't fit together properly.

Begin by cutting the plywood for the bed box to size (see Plywood Cutting Guide, above). Cut plywood for the front panels (pieces 1 and 2), and then cut solid stock for the bed frame ends and sides (pieces 3 through 5).

For help with alignment, use dowels or biscuits to join the three front panels together. Drill or cut the joints, depending on the method you prefer, and then glue the three panels edge-to-edge, as shown in the drawings on page 112. For clamping these large assemblies, I bought 7'-long pipes to use with my pipe clamp fixtures. Clean up any glue squeeze-out, and then apply pressure-sensitive edge banding (pieces 6) to all but the desk opening edges of the assembly (see Figure 1 on page 111). Trim the excess banding off with a mill file.

With the front panels joined together, lay out the two foot openings, as shown in the drawings on page 112. Then, cut them with a jigsaw after drilling access holes in the corners for inserting the saw blade.

Join the four pieces of the bed frame with counterbored screws (pieces 7), lapping the end pieces over the side pieces, and fill the counterbores with oak plugs (pieces 8). Then, drill holes in the ends for installing the bed hardware brackets (see the drawing on the top of page 112).

The ribbing (pieces 9), which reinforces the bed box to give it rigidity, is made with plywood scraps and secondary wood. Rip 1½"-wide strips for all the pieces, and then glue and screw some of them into L-brackets for the vertical ribs. Now, build a ribbing framework to fit inside the bed frame,

Cabinet Detail

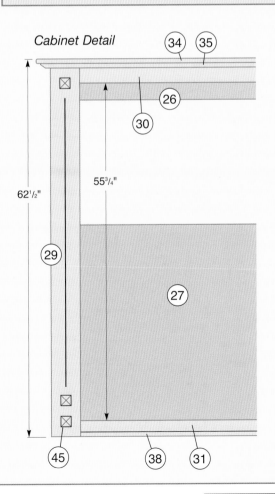

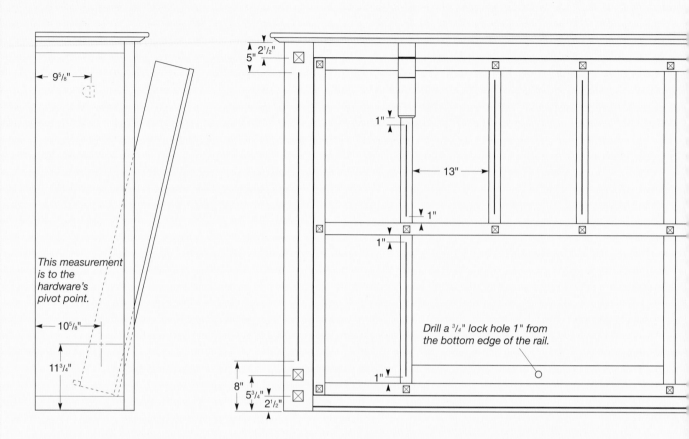

This measurement is to the hardware's pivot point.

Drill a ³⁄₄" lock hole 1" from the bottom edge of the rail.

Material List

(Continued from page 113.)

	T x W x L			T x W x L
17 Desk Rail (1)	¾" x 3¾" x 43"		**32** Stiffeners (8)	¾" x 2¾" x 141¹¹⁄₁₆"
18 Cam Lock (1)	¾" Cylinder		**33** Caps (4)	¾" x 3½" x 15⅜"
19 Dowel Pins (2)	¼" Dia. x 1¼"		**34** Top Edging (1)	¾" x 3⅜" x 140"
20 Desk Hinge (1)	1½" x 43"		**35** Front Trim Molding (1)	¾" x 3¼" x 96"
21 Desk Support Hinges (2)	1½" x 6"		**36** Side Trim Moldings (2)	¾" x 3¼" x 20"
22 Desk Stops (2)	¾" x 1⅜" x 1⅜"		**37** Side Moldings (4)	½" x 3⅜" x 16"
23 Sides (2)	¾" x 15½" x 61"		**38** Base Shoe (1)	½" x ¾" x 77⅞"
24 Upper Mounting Plates (2)	¾" x 14¾" x 5¾"		**39** Baseboard Backer (1)	¾" x 2½" x 77⅞"
25 Lower Mounting Plates (2)	¾" x 14¾" x 34¾"		**40** Bolster Blocks (2)	1¼" x 2⅝" x 3"
26 Upper Brace (1)	¾" x 5¾" x 84½"		**41** Rails and Stiles (6)	¼" x 2" x 96"
27 Lower Brace (1)	¾" x 34¾" x 84½"		**42** Top Supports (2)	1¾" x 3" x 2½"
28 Top (1)	¾" x 16⅜" x 86"		**43** Top Supports (2)	¾" x 3" x 3¼"
29 Columns (2)	1¾" x 5" x 61"		**44** Small Squares (14)	1¼" x 1¼" x 6"
30 Top Rail (1)	¾" x 2½" x 77⅞"		**45** Large Squares (6)	1¾" x 1¾" x 6"
31 Baseboard (1)	¾" x 2¾" x 77⅞"		**46** Inside Panel (1)	¾" x 48" x 75"
			47 Inside Panel (1)	¾" x 6" x 75"

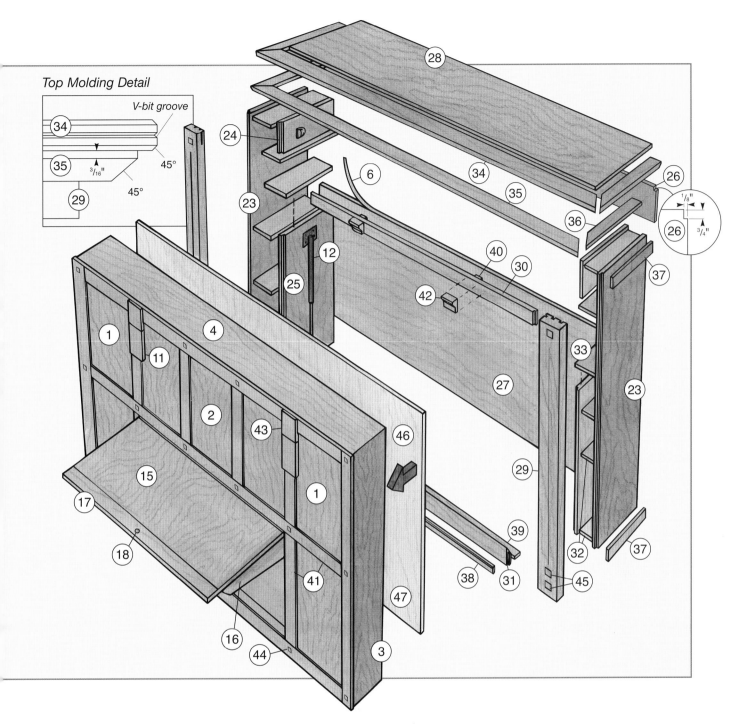

Top Molding Detail

V-bit groove

45°

45°

³/₁₆"

¹/₈"

³/₄"

countersinking screws (pieces 7) to hold it together. With this framework done, slip it into the bed frame, and use screws (pieces 10) to join the two subassemblies.

Securing the bed frame and ribbing to the front panel assembly is a big job that requires two people. First, lay the panel face-side down on the floor, and then position the bed frame on it to drill your pilot holes. Make sure the frame is flush with the bottom edge of the panel and exposes a ¼" plywood reveal at

each end. Next, turn over the frame, and spread glue on all its bottom edges. Then, reposition the frame on the panel, and drive in the screws (pieces 10).

More Bed Box Details

With the basic bed box made, now you can take care of several small details before moving on to the cabinet construction. Cut the feet (pieces 11) to size, and chamfer the edges, as shown in the foot detail drawing on page 112.

Next, install the special hinges that come with the fold-down hardware (pieces 12). Center the hinges in the foot holes, and screw them to the ribbing above. Then, bore a ⅜" hole through the ribbing and the bed frame for each locking pin (see Figure 2 on page 116). To complete the hinge installation, have a helper hold the feet in position on the front panel while you secure the hinges. (See the hardware instructions for more on the hinge and foot installation.)

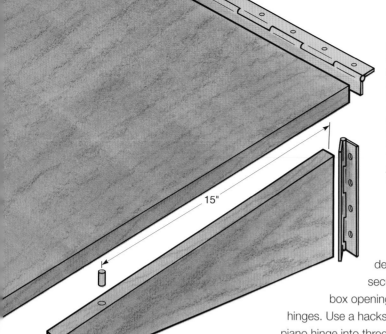

Figure 3: *The bottom edge of each desk support tapers 10°, and the front end is cut at 45°. After banding all the edges of the supports, install a ¼"-diameter x 1¼"-long locking pin in the top edge of each support.*

15"

For a finished look, frame the desk opening with oak boards (piece 13). However, first install a ½"-thick filler strip of scrap wood (piece 14) in the space at the bottom of the opening so the frame pieces come out even. After gluing in the filler strip, cut the frame stock to length, and glue the pieces around the opening. Use finish nails to hold the stock while the glue sets.

Now, cut plywood for the desk (piece 15) and desk supports (pieces 16). Once you have the stock for the desk supports cut out, band saw the pieces to shape, following the guidelines in Figure 3. Clean up the edges, and apply pressure-sensitive edge banding to all the support edges, as well as to the top and side edges of the desk. For the bottom edge of the desk, glue on a protective oak rail (piece 17). When the glue has dried, center a ¾"-diameter hole for the cam lock (piece 18), as shown in the drawing on page 114.

Pinning the desk supports to the desk will keep these pieces from sagging while you write (see Figure 3). Glue a pin (pieces 19) into a 1"-deep hole in each support. Then, in a few minutes, after the desk and supports have been installed in the bed, drill ⅜"-deep holes in the underside of the desk to align with the pins.

The desk and desk supports are secured in the bed box opening with piano hinges. Use a hacksaw to cut the long piano hinge into three sections (pieces 20 and 21), and then screw each hinge to the appropriate edge of each plywood piece. With a friend's help, hold the desk in the bed box opening, and drill pilot holes for the desk hinge (in the closed position, the desk should be flush with the front panel assembly). Secure the desk, and then do the same thing with the supports, which should be positioned 2" from the bed box opening wall and should hold the desk level with the floor. Wrap up this step by drilling the pin holes in the underside of the desk.

Glue the desk stops (pieces 22) in the lower corners of the desk opening, and cut a biscuit slot for the lock arm to swing into.

Figure 2: *Secure each special hinge to the ribbing, and drill a hole so the locking pin passes through the frame to hold the bed in the closed position.*

Constructing the Cabinet

Just as with the bed box, begin building the cabinet by cutting the plywood parts (pieces 23 through 28), referring to the cutting guide on page 113. Be sure to cut notches in the upper brace (piece 26), as shown in the drawing on page 115. Once the plywood has been cut, rip 1¾"-thick oak for the front columns (pieces 29) and some ¾" oak for the top rail (piece 30) and baseboard (piece 31).

The columns join the mounting plates, sides, top rail, and baseboard with tongue-and-groove joints. Referring to the drawing on page 112, rout ¼"-deep grooves in the columns with a ⅜" straight bit and a straightedge guide. After routing these grooves, rout a V-groove on the front of each column.

The tongues on all the plywood pieces should be cut flush to their back sides, while the top rail and baseboard have centered tongues. To cut all the tongues, use a ¼" dado blade, and be sure to clamp a wood face to your table saw fence to protect it from the blade during this operation.

Now, glue the plywood pieces to the columns, and cut stiffeners (pieces 32) to butt glue between each mounting plate and the sides. (Note that the upper mounting plates should stick out above the columns by ¾"—this will be covered by the trim molding later.) The stiffeners are simply butt glued into place.

Once each side assembly has been joined, drill the bracket installation holes in the lower mounting plates (see the drawing on page 114, left). Then, install the brackets on the lower mounting plates and on the ends of the bed frame, and give your friend a holler. With help, place the cabinet side assemblies against the bed frame, and hook up the hardware; then, glue the top rail to the columns. Using long clamps to hold everything together, position the braces, and drill counterbored pilot holes for mounting them to the cabinet. Spread glue on all these butt joints, and screw the pieces down. Fill the counterbores with oak plugs, and sand them flush.

Next, cut the cavity caps (pieces 33), and glue them to cover the ends of each cavity, using a few finish nails to hold them in place while the glue dries. Then, apply pressure-sensitive banding to the exposed edges of the braces.

Rout all the molding (pieces 34 through 38) using the bits shown in the drawing on page 115, top left. On narrow molding such as the base shoe, it's always best to rout the edge of a wider board first and then rip the molded edge off afterward. Miter the edging, and glue it to the top. Then, miter the trim molding to length, and construct a three-sided frame using biscuits to strengthen the corners. Position the trim molding frame on top of the cabinet so it slips into the notches, and screw it to the pieces below. Next, position the top on the trim molding frame, and secure it with counterbored screws. Fill the holes with oak plugs, and then glue and nail the side molding to the cabinet sides.

Since the baseboard is long and slender, reinforce it with a backer strip (piece 39) made from scrap. Glue the backer behind the baseboard to form an L-bracket. When the glue has dried, tip the carcass back a bit to glue the baseboard assembly into the grooves in the columns, and install the base shoe.

Complete the cabinet construction by installing the pistons and connecting them to the bed frame, and then install the stops supplied with the hardware kit (see Figure 4). Once the stops are in, glue bolster blocks (pieces 40) to the inside of the top rail where the locking pins are located. These blocks bear against the locking pins to keep the bed closed tight (see Figure 5).

Figure 4: *The stops should be screwed to the upper mounting plates to keep the bed box flush with the front of the cabinet.*

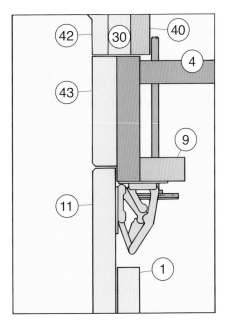

Figure 5: *In its closed position, the special hinge locks the bed to the cabinet. Pulling out the foot will release the lock and allow you to open the bed.*

Completing the Cabinet Face

The work remaining on this project is mostly decorative. Rip plenty of ¼" stock for the rails and stiles (pieces 41), and then cut the pieces to fit on the cabinet, as shown in the exploded view on page 115. Once they've been cut to length, rout a shallow V-groove in the center of the appropriate pieces, and then glue and nail the pieces to the front panels. Cut the decorative supports (pieces 42 and 43), as well, and glue them to the box above the feet.

The squares (pieces 44 and 45) can easily be made on the table saw. Rip seven pieces of 1¼" x 1¼" x 6" oak stock, and three pieces of 1¾" x 1¾" x 6" oak. Then, tilt the saw blade 10° to cut both ends of each piece into a pyramid (see the drawings on page 114). Next, cut off the squares, and fasten them to the cabinet front with epoxy.

The final plywood panels are for the inside skin of the bed (pieces 46 and 47). Cut the pieces, and secure them to the ribbing with counterbored screws. Then, plug the holes, and sand them flush.

Believe it or not, the time has come to sand and finish the fold-down bed. Sand the entire project to 180 grit, and ease all the sharp edges. I finished the project with Watco natural stain and then sprayed it with lacquer. Be sure to wear a respirator when spraying lacquer. If you don't have spray equipment, use a brush-on lacquer, such as Deft, or choose a polyurethane varnish instead.

When the finishing is complete, reinstall the desk pieces and the hardware. Now, get lots of help to move this heavy load into position, and once it's in place, be sure to screw the carcass to the studs in your wall with long deck screws.

Using the Bed

You'll find that once the mattress is installed, this bed hardware is easy to use and trouble free. The weight of the mattress equalizes the swing speed of the mechanism and reduces the effort needed to open the bed. You'll also notice how different the hardware looks from the kind of fold-down contraptions you've seen in the past. With this hardware, you can rest easy—there's no danger of reenacting a Laurel and Hardy routine in which they end up squished against the wall when their bed unexpectedly swings closed.

Trundle Bed

You're always ready for overnight company with this modern twist on the time-honored trundle. Simple bed hardware and ultralarge slides make it sturdy, while a sailboat-inspired design gives it a great updated look. Plus, those little ones can actually get a good night's rest in this bed, whether sleeping on the extralong, full-size upper bunk or the regular-twin-size trundle.

by Rick White

Trundle beds are great space savers and the ultimate in practicality, but pushing and pulling that large, unwieldy trundle can be challenging. The trundle, even when it has wheels, can twist or skew out of alignment and get stuck. I solved that problem with a pair of extra-large slides. The casters on the bottom of the trundle support the weight, and the slides keep the trundle straight. I was tempted to use the slides alone, but the manufacturer made it clear that they were "not designed to carry human weight."

This bed's nautical design inspiration came from a 40' sailboat owned by a friend of mine. The project is easy to make and looks great. I made mine out of mahogany and sized it to last well beyond the grade school

years—while the trundle has a twin mattress, the upper bunk features an extralong, full mattress (see Figure 1).

Starting with the Ends

You'll invest the lion's share of the work in the two identical ends of the bed, so it's best to start there. Referring to the Material List on page 122, cut the pieces of the end subassemblies

(pieces 1 through 5) to size. Next, use a dado set to plow stopped grooves in the appropriate edges of the corner posts (you'll create right and left pieces at this time), and then square up the groove ends with a chisel. (Look to the drawings throughout this article for construction details.) Use the same dado head to form the matching tongues on the end panels. The upper

Figure 1: *The beauty of a trundle bed is that you get two beds packed in the space of one. This bed is sized to last a child well beyond grade school, with a top bunk that features an extralong, full-size mattress.*

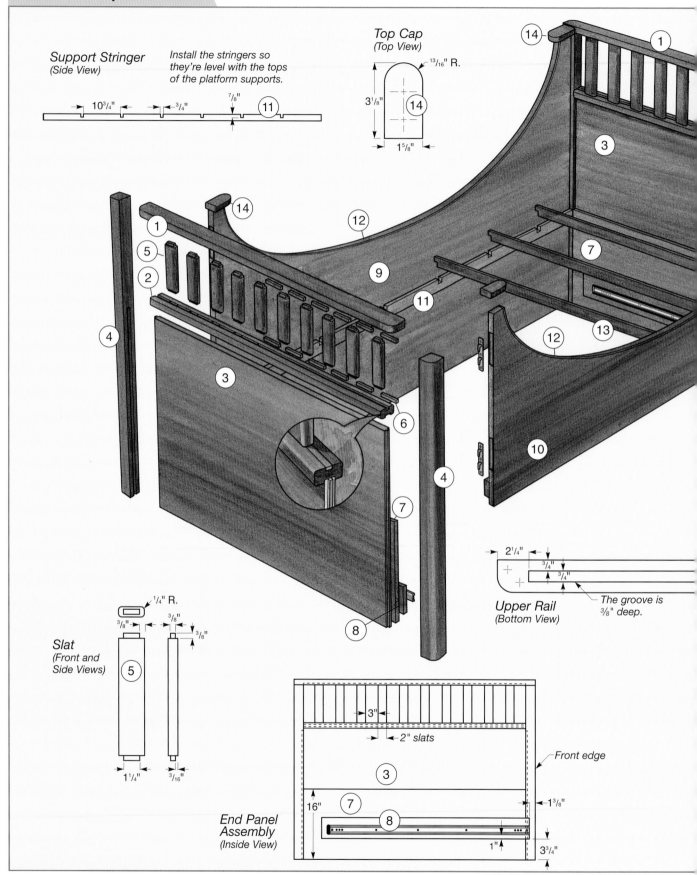

Support Stringer
(Side View)

Install the stringers so they're level with the tops of the platform supports.

10³/₄"   ³/₄"   ⁷/₈"   11

Top Cap
(Top View)

¹³/₁₆" R.

3¹/₈"   14

1⁵/₈"

Top Cap (Top View)

14   1

3

12   7

1

14

5

2   9   11

4   12   13

3   10

6

7

8   4

Upper Rail
(Bottom View)

2¹/₄"   ³/₄"   ³/₄"

The groove is ³/₈" deep.

Slat
(Front and
Side Views)

¹/₄" R.

³/₈"   ³/₈"   ³/₈"

5

1¹/₄"   ³/₁₆"

End Panel
Assembly
(Inside View)

3"

2" slats

Front edge

3

16"   7

8   1³/₈"

1"   3³/₄"

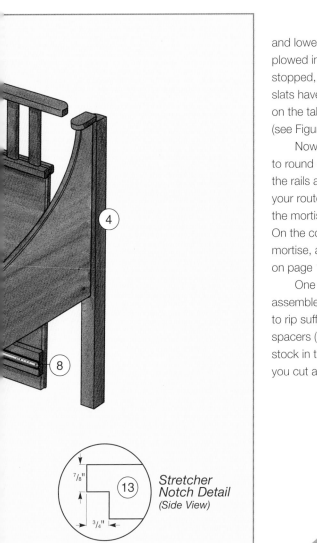

and lower rails also have grooves plowed into them (the uppers' are stopped, the lowers' are through). The slats have tenons on both ends, formed on the table saw using a tenoning jig (see Figure 2).

Now, turn to your handheld router to round over the appropriate edges of the rails and slats. As long as you have your router out, go ahead and form the mortises for the bed rail hardware. On the corner posts, this is a two-level mortise, as shown in the post drawings on page 123.

One task remains before you can assemble the two bed ends: You need to rip sufficient stock for the slat spacers (pieces 6). Test fit the spacer stock in the grooves in the rails before you cut all the spacers to length. The

grooves house the slat tenons, and the spacers hold the slats in place and fill in the grooves.

Assembling the Ends

As you should always do, test fit all the end pieces together to be certain you are ready for glue-up. When they all fit, start with the rail and slat sub-assemblies. To ensure symmetrical placement of the slats, glue a spacer dead center in each rail groove, and then glue the slats and spacers in place, starting in the center and moving outward. Once the glue has cured, you can trim off any excess length on the outer spacers. Now, attach the rail and slat subassemblies to the plywood end panels with glue and clamps. The last step is to glue the posts to the

Figure 2: *The slats on the bed ends have tenons that fit into grooves on the upper and lower rails. Form the tenons on your table saw using a tenoning jig.*

Stretcher Notch Detail (Side View)

subassemblies you've just created. I drove screws through the top rail into the posts for extra strength, plugged the holes, and sanded the plugs flush.

Next, make the platform and slide supports (pieces 7 and 8). Notice that the combination of these parts forms a buildup to ensure that the lower trundle box will clear the bed frame on the slides. Attach these parts to the inside of the bed ends with glue and screws, as shown in the exploded drawing on page 120. A final sanding is all that is needed to complete the two bed ends.

Forming the Side Panels

The front and back side panels (pieces 9 and 10) are made of plywood. Cut them to size now, and while you're at it, cut your support stringers (pieces 11) and the edging (pieces 12) that's used to cover the horizontal plywood edges.

Once you have these pieces cut to size, lay out the long, curved cutouts on the two side panels (for the dimensions, see the scaled drawing of the curve at right). Use a jigsaw to cut the curve exactly on the line. Then, use the waste pieces as clamping forms to glue the edging in place (see Figure 3 on page 124).

While the glue is curing, use the drawings on pages 120–121 to help you lay out the notches on the bed support stringers and stretchers (pieces 13). I formed the notches on a band saw. Also use the band saw to cut the curved ends of the top caps (pieces 14), and then step to the belt sander to clean up the cut (see Figure 4 on page 124).

As soon as you remove the clamps from the side panels, sand the edgings flush, and trim the ends flush, too. Attach the bed support stringers and top caps to the sides with screws and glue (see Figure 5 on page 125), and plug the screw holes on the top caps.

Trundle Exploded View

Side Panel and Lower Face Curves

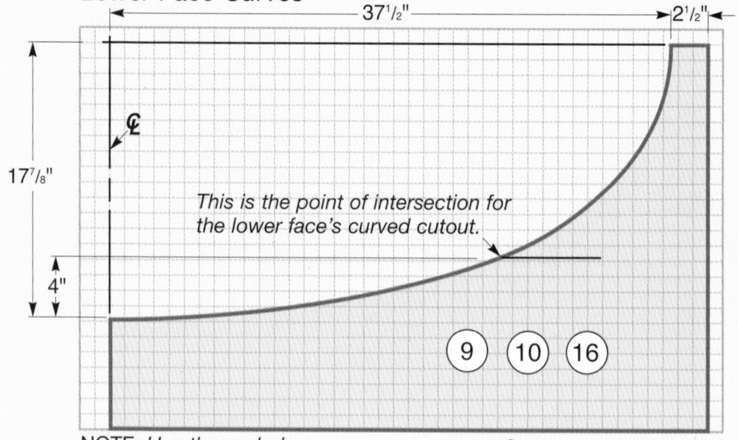

37½"
2½"
17⅞"
4"
℄
This is the point of intersection for the lower face's curved cutout.
9
10
16

NOTE: *Use the scaled drawing above to lay out the curved cutouts on the side panels and lower face.*

One square equals 1".

Material List

		T x W x L
1	Upper Rails (2)	1¼" x 2¼" x 57"
2	Lower Rails (2)	1¼" x 2¾" x 52½"
3	End Panels (2)	¾" x 29¾" x 53¼"
4	Corner Posts (4)	2¼" x 2¼" x 39¾"
5	Slats (20)	¾" x 2" x 9⅛"
6	Slat Spacers (44)	⅜" x ⅜" x 3¾"
7	Platform Supports (2)	¾" x 16" x 52½"
8	Slide Supports (2)	1" x 4¾" x 49"
9	Side Panel, Back (1)	¾" x 39¾" x 80"
10	Side Panel, Front (1)	¾" x 25¾" x 80"
11	Support Stringers (2)	¾" x 1¾" x 80"
12	Edging (2)	⅛" x ⅞" x 270"
13	Stretchers (6)	¾" x 1¾" x 54"
14	Top Caps (4)	1" x 1⅝" x 3⅛"
15	Upper Bed Platform (1)	¾" x 54" x 81½"
16	Lower Face (1)	¾" x 13⅜" x 79 9/16"
17	Plyedge (1)	1/16" x ⅞" x 28"
18	Lower Box Sides (2)	¾" x 13⅜" x 46"
19	Lower Box Back (1)	¾" x 13⅞" x 75"
20	Lower Bed Platform (1)	¾" x 38½" x 75"
21	Corner Glue Blocks (4)	¾" x ¾" x 2⅛"
22	Cross Supports (8)	¾" x 1⅞" x 37"
23	Long Supports (2)	¾" x 1⅞" x 75"

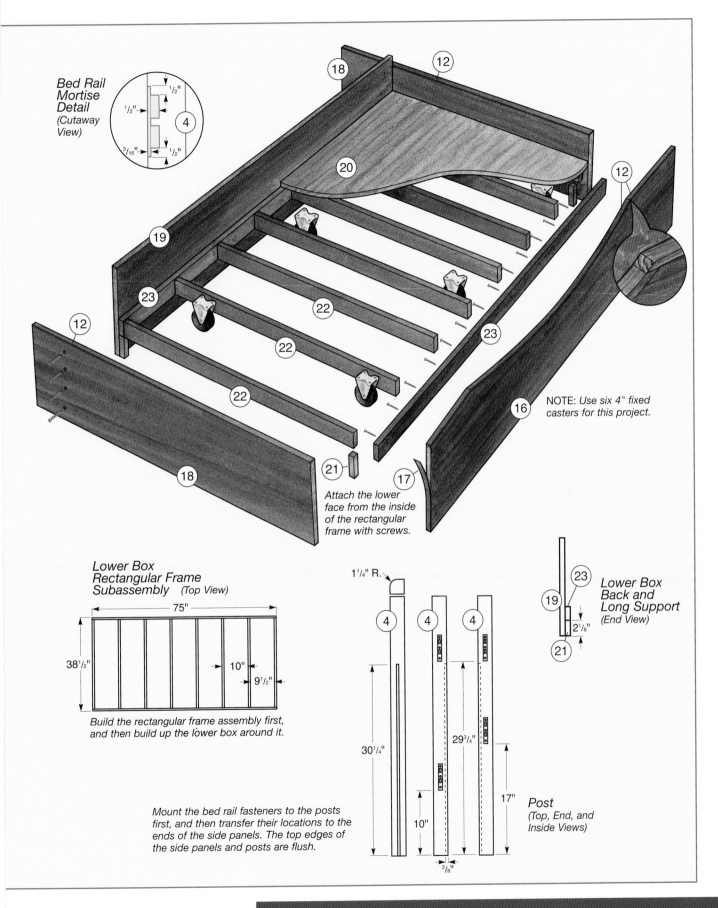

Bed Rail Mortise Detail *(Cutaway View)*

1/2"
1/2"
4
3/16"
1/2"

18
12
20
19
23
22
22
22
23
21
12
16
12
17

NOTE: *Use six 4" fixed casters for this project.*

Attach the lower face from the inside of the rectangular frame with screws.

18

Lower Box Rectangular Frame Subassembly *(Top View)*

75"
38 1/2"
10"
9 1/2"

Build the rectangular frame assembly first, and then build up the lower box around it.

Mount the bed rail fasteners to the posts first, and then transfer their locations to the ends of the side panels. The top edges of the side panels and posts are flush.

1 1/4" R.
4
4
4

30 1/4"
29 3/4"
17"
10"
3/8"

Post *(Top, End, and Inside Views)*

23
19
21

2 1/8"

Lower Box Back and Long Support *(End View)*

Bed for Readers

This queen-size bed features a perfectly inclined backrest, three large storage compartments, and three drawers for your bedside collectibles. The crowning touch: Open the middle drawer and drop the support down to make a rock-solid resting place for that steaming mug of tea.

by Rick White

There's an old adage that says, "The longer your years, the shorter your days." Whether you consider yourself over the hill or not, life just seems to get busier as the years pass. If the only quiet time you have to catch up on reading is late at night when the kids are asleep, you'll love this project.

Most beds are designed for lying down, not sitting up and reading. Plus, few styles offer convenient storage for all the catalogs, books, and magazines you may need to get through. Even bedside tables offer limited storage space for reading material.

This multiple-use queen-size bed addresses these problems. It features both comfortable back support for reading and lots of storage. Another key feature: It has flip-down doors that are supported by the pull-out drawers; the backs of the doors then become small but sturdy tables to hold books, popcorn bowls, or maybe even a remote control if you surf the channels instead of reading yourself to sleep.

Simple Headboard Cabinet Design

The headboard is essentially a plywood cabinet with nine separate compartments. This subassembly is secured between two legs and topped off with a gently curved pediment made of walnut and ash.

You'll want to check out the drawings throughout this article for construction details. Then, begin building the cabinet by cutting the sides, dividers, top, shelves, and bottom (pieces 1 through 6) to size, referring to the Material List on page 131 for dimensions. As this is hardwood-veneered plywood, make the straight cuts with a fine-toothed plywood blade on the table saw to minimize splintering the veneer. Keep the best-looking side of each panel facing up as you cut—the tearout will occur when the blade exits the workpiece.

Now, grab your router and straight bit to plow three ³⁄₁₆"-deep dadoes across each side and four across each divider (two on each side), as shown in Figure 1. As the drawings show, these are all through cuts. Once they've been made, adjust the bit depth to ¼" to create stopped rabbets along the back edge of each side and the top, to accommodate the back. With the routing completed, lay out the angled front edges of the sides and dividers. Trim the angled cuts close to your line with a jigsaw. Then, clamp on a straightedge, and clean up these edges with a ¾" straight bit chucked in your portable router, as shown in Figure 2 on page 128.

Dry fit the cabinet together, and then mill enough cap stock (piece 7) to trim the front edges of all the cabinet parts. This is just square stock, ripped and planed to size.

Assemble the cabinet with glue and clamps, making sure that it's flat and square. When the glue has dried, miter the cap stock to fit, and apply it to the cabinet with glue and finish nails. Be sure to install the vertical strips first. Predrill pilot holes in the hardwood for the nails, and set the nail heads below the surface. The last trim to apply is the upper shelf trim (piece 8), which helps frame the drawer openings. Cover all the holes with matching filler, and sand it smooth after it has dried.

The plywood back (piece 9) and the lower panels (pieces 10 and 11) close up

Figure 1: *The dadoes for the headboard's straightforward joinery are plowed while the sides and dividers are still rectangular. Angled front edges are laid out and cut next.*

Figure 2: *For the angled front edges of the sides and dividers, first cut close to the layout lines with a handheld jigsaw (above). Then, trim the angled edges smooth and straight using a router with a straight bit and a straightedge jig (left).*

the headboard. Attach panel cleats (piece 12), setting them ⅞" in from the front of the headboard, and secure the panels with glue and screws. Fit the back into its rabbet, and attach it with brads.

Laminated Legs

The two headboard legs are created by laminating pieces of ash lumber to a ½"-thick walnut core. Face glue and

Figure 3: *Glue the leg laminations together, holding the parts with plenty of clamps until the glue sets. Check the joint initially to remedy any glue creeping.*

clamp one long ash lamination (pieces 13) to each of the walnut laminations (pieces 14). After the glue has dried, glue and clamp the two short ash laminations (pieces 15 and 16) to the other side of each leg (see Figure 3).

When dry, run each assembled leg across the jointer. Later, you'll need to form a gentle curve onto the top of each leg to mate the legs to the arched pediment.

Graceful Arched Pediment

The curved tops of the headboard and footboard (the pediments) are built up with a series of five ⅜"-thick ash laminations (pieces 17) that are glued together in a plywood form. A sixth walnut lamination (pieces 18) will be installed after the pediments have been secured to the legs.

A bending form forces each lamination into an arched shape and holds them all tightly together while the glue dries. After you rip and crosscut all 12 laminations to size, refer to Curved

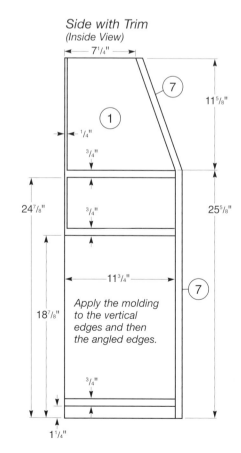

Side with Trim
(Inside View)

7¼"

7

11⅝"

1

¼"

¾"

24⅞"

¾"

25⅝"

11¾"

7

18⅞"

Apply the molding to the vertical edges and then the angled edges.

¾"

1¼"

Laminations at right for directions on building your form. Then, apply a liberal amount of adhesive between five of the ash laminations, and clamp them in place securely.

When the adhesive has dried, scrape off the excess, and pass one edge of the pediment across the jointer. Set your table saw fence so it's 6⁵⁄₁₆" from a sharp ripping blade, and rip the pediment to width. (You may need a helper for this task—the pediment is a handful.) Then, pass the ripped edge across the jointer, reducing the part to its final 6¼" width. Crosscut it to 68½" long (measuring along the curve), and then chamfer the bottom edge with a 45° bearing-guided chamfering bit. Run the bearing along the bottom face of the pediment so the router can ride the jointed sides (rather than have to follow the curve). Using several passes, shape the ends first and then the sides; this will eliminate any tearout from cutting across the grain on the ends. Before moving on, repeat this process to create the footboard pediment—it's identical to the headboard pediment.

Now, clamp the legs temporarily in place on the headboard. Center one of the pediments on the two legs, and trace its curve onto the face of the legs. Remove the legs, and step to the band saw to cut the ends of each leg to the curved layout lines. Sand the curves smooth and exactly to the lines on a stationary disc sander. When the curves on the pediment and legs are a perfect match, glue and clamp the legs in place on the headboard.

Grab the arched pediment and position it on the headboard subassembly. Mark the leg locations on its underside, and bore pilot holes through the piece. Then, predrill for the 3½"-long lag bolts (pieces 19), and attach the pediment to the legs. The reason you're using such large bolts is that people are bound to use the arched pediments as handles to lift the bed, so these joints will be subject to some serious stress. Countersink for the bolt

Curved Laminations

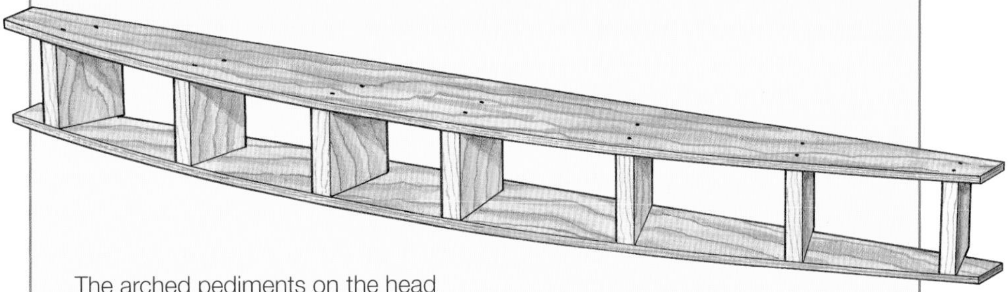

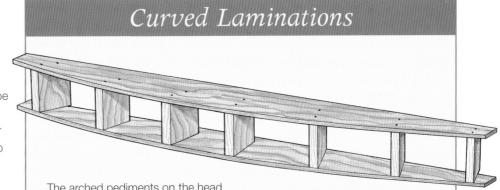

The arched pediments on the head and foot of the bed are created by gluing hardwood laminations together while clamped to a curved form. Make the form from plywood shaped and mounted to dimension lumber with glue and screws. It is important that the form's curve be fair and true. To form the curve on your jig (see the pediment jig drawing on page 130), mark the endpoints and centerpoint, and flex a thin strip of hardboard to lay out the shape. Use a belt sander to smooth out the long, gentle arc. The form also needs to provide good purchase for the many clamps it takes to apply even pressure to this pediment buildup. If you're limited to using shorter clamps, make some clamp cutouts, as shown in the pediment jig drawing.

The type of adhesive to use is a significant consideration for this task. White or yellow woodworking glues may work, but their elasticity could allow the curve to creep and change shape, even after the glue cures. Epoxy is a better choice for this operation—specifically, a mixture with a long open time. The open time not only provides enough time to place the laminations around the form and clamp them properly, but it also allows the resin to infiltrate the wood fibers, thus creating a stronger bond. If epoxy isn't a reasonable option for you, polyurethane glue is another good choice for dry-bent laminations.

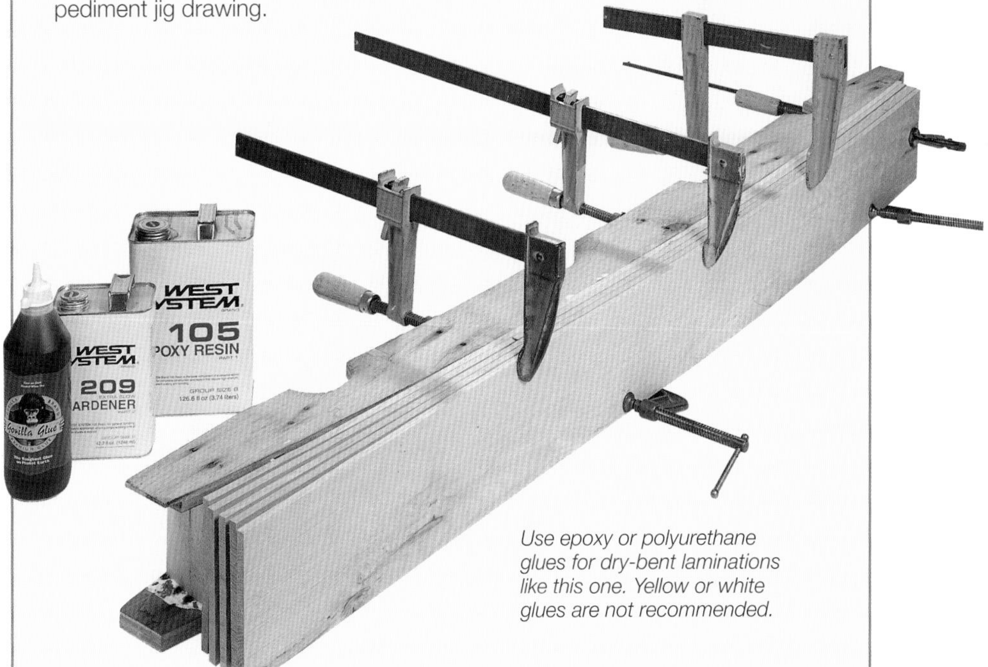

Use epoxy or polyurethane glues for dry-bent laminations like this one. Yellow or white glues are not recommended.

Pediment Jig
(Top View)

$3^{3}/_{4}$"

Clamping cutouts (optional)

$36^{3}/_{4}$"

18

19

17

3

15

41

2

9

2

14

4

5

13

8

8

1

4

32

4

8

5

4

7

10

11

29

10

12

7

16

12

7

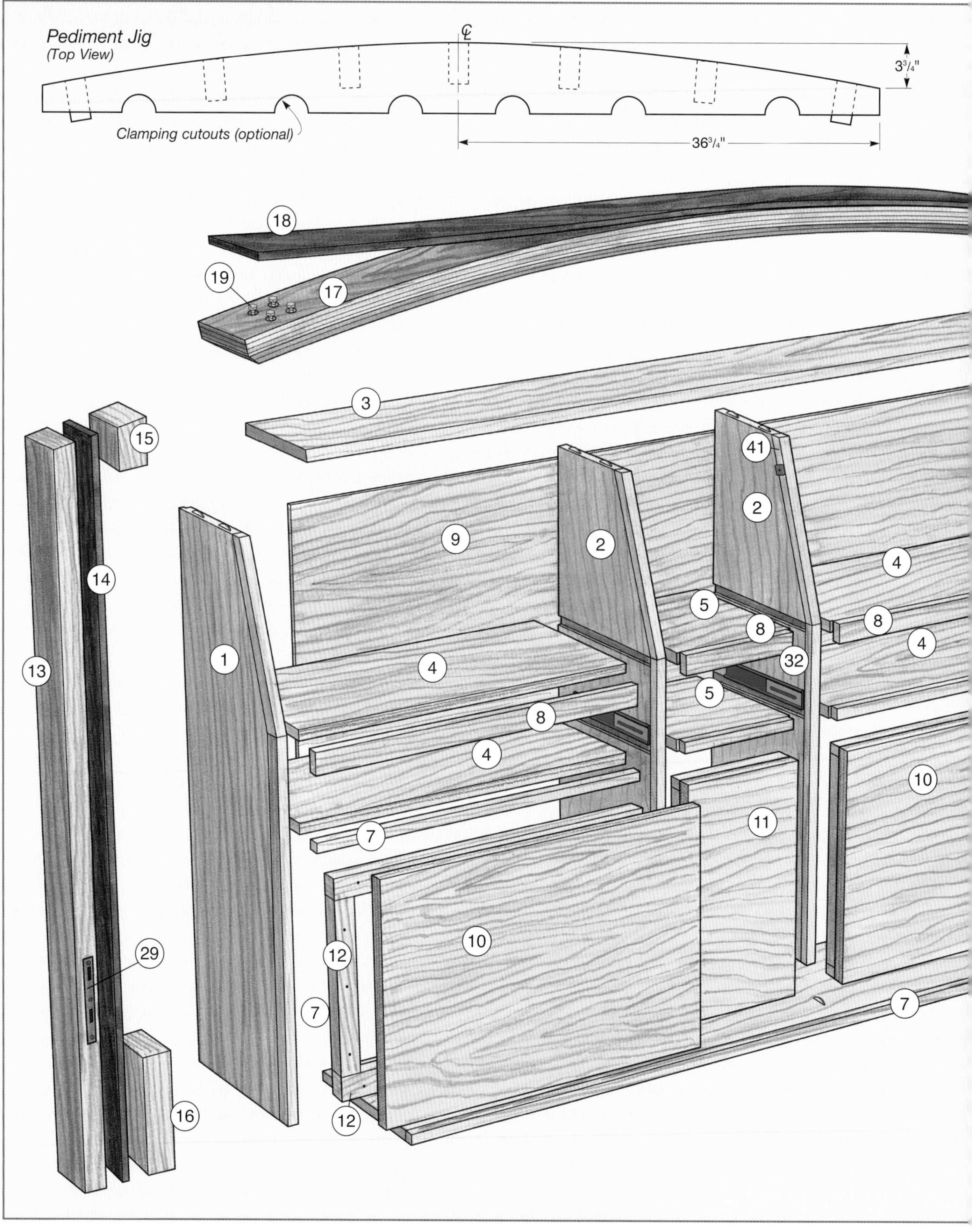

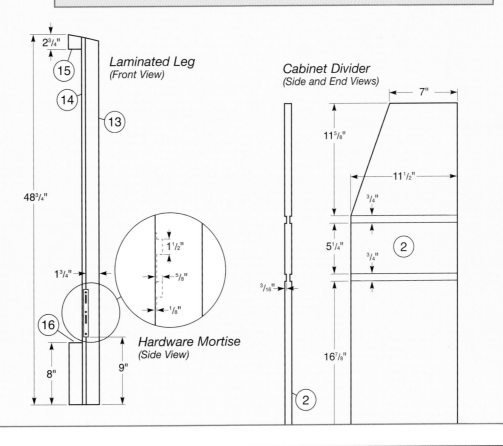

Material List – Headboard

		T x W x L
1	Cabinet Sides (2)	¾" x 11¾" x 37¼"
2	Cabinet Dividers (2)	¾" x 11½" x 35¼"
3	Cabinet Top (1)	¾" x 8¼" x 61¼"
4	Cabinet Large Shelves (4)	¾" x 11½" x 25"
5	Cabinet Small Shelves (2)	¾" x 11½" x 9⅜"
6	Cabinet Bottom (1)	¾" x 11¾" x 60⅛"
7	Cap Stock Molding (1)	¾" x ¾" x 350"
8	Upper Shelf Trim (1)	¾" x 1¾" x 60"
9	Cabinet Back (1)	¾" x 18⅞" x 60¾"
10	Large Lower Panels (2)	¾" x 16⅞" x 60⅝"
11	Small Lower Panel (1)	¾" x 16⅞" x 9"
12	Panel Cleating (1)	¾" x 1½" x 210"
13	Long Leg Outside Laminations (2)	1¾" x 4" x 48¾"
14	Long Leg Center Laminations (2)	½" x 4" x 48¾"
15	Upper Long Leg Inside Laminations (2)	2¾" x 4" x 2¾"
16	Lower Long Leg Inside Laminations (2)	1¾" x 4" x 8"
17	Pediment Ash Laminations* (10)	⅜" x 1⅜" x 72"
18	Pediment Walnut Laminations* (2)	⅜" x 6⅜" x 72"
19	Lag Bolts (16)	⅜" Dia. x 3½"

Sufficient material for headboard and footboard pediments.

2¾"

Laminated Leg
(Front View)

Cabinet Divider
(Side and End Views)

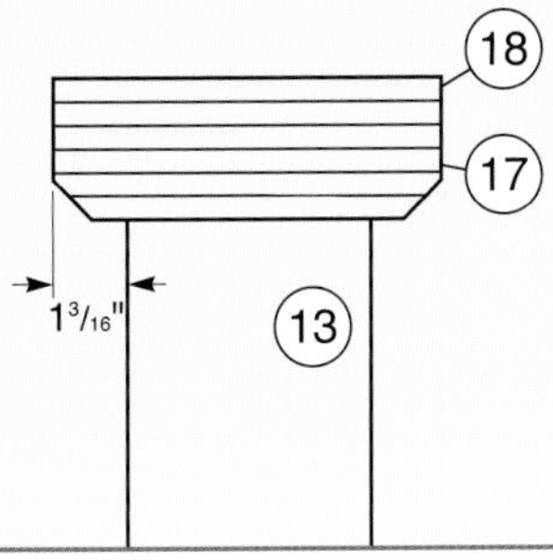

7"

11⅝"

11½"

¾"

5¼"

¾"

⑮

⑭

⑬

②

48¾"

1¾"

③/16"

16⅞"

1½"

⅝"

⅛"

⑯

Hardware Mortise
(Side View)

⑱

⑰

⑬

1³/16"

⑬

8"

9"

②

②

heads, making sure they are below the surface before you proceed to the next step (see Figure 4).

Wrap up by gluing and clamping the final (walnut) lamination in place. After the glue has dried, use a bearing-guided, laminate-trimming bit to pare the edges flush with the ash. Sand the edges, and you're ready to move on to the footboard.

Solid-Ash and Walnut Footboard

The only difference between the headboard and footboard (aside from height) is that the latter sports a couple of hardwood panels instead of a cabinet. Refer to the Material List on page 133, and then begin construction with the legs. Face glue and clamp two ash laminations (pieces 20) around a walnut one (pieces 21), and dress the assembled leg on the jointer after the glue has dried. Do this for each leg, and then crosscut them to length. On the router table, plow stopped mortises into the inside faces of the legs, and square up the ends of each mortise with a chisel.

Edge glue hardwood stock to make the footboard panels (pieces 22 and 23), paying attention to the grain pattern. Size the panels to create the upper and lower sections, and then plow a ½" groove along the joining edges. Cut the curved shape on the upper panel's edge, as shown in the elevation drawings. Mill the ½" x ½" tenons onto the panels' ends with a dado blade in the table saw. Mill the decorative walnut strip (piece 24) that

Figure 4: *Heavy-duty lag bolts ensure that the arched pediments will not come loose from the bed's legs. Make sure you sink the heads below the level of the arch.*

fits between the upper and lower panels to size. Sand both panels and the walnut strip to 180 grit, and then glue and clamp the panel subassembly between the legs to complete the footboard.

Attach the footboard pediment (which you made earlier) in exactly the same fashion as the headboard version. Apply the final walnut lamination, clean up any glue squeeze-out, and sand the edges smooth.

Side Rails and Moldings

There isn't much to the side rail assemblies: They're just a couple of lengths of molding (pieces 25) attached to boards (pieces 26). Rip the moldings to size, and then lay out the five dadoes in each at the locations shown in the side rail and molding drawing at right. Make the dado cuts with the aid of your miter gauge. Glue the walnut accent strip (pieces 27) to the top edge of each rail. After sanding the rails, screw and glue the moldings to them.

Form five lengths of stock to serve as the rail slats (pieces 28). These fit into the dadoes in the side rail moldings and will support your box spring once the bed is assembled. Now, you're ready to attach the rails to the headboard and footboard. This is done with bed frame hardware designed specifically for this application (pieces 29). It's strong and totally invisible, and it allows for disassembly when you need to move the bed elsewhere (see Figure 5 on page 134).

Three Drawers for Storage

This bed features three 12"-deep drawers, two of which are ideal for storing stationery and reading materials. The third, smaller drawer is designed for reading glasses, pens, and similar items.

Referring to the Material List on page 134, cut the drawer fronts, backs, and sides (pieces 30 through 32) to size. Then, chuck a ¼" straight bit in the router table, and plow a through groove in each part for the drawer bottoms (pieces 33 and 34), as shown in the drawer

Footboard
(Inside and Side Views)

1³/₄"

9"

24

27

26

Footboard Panels
(Front View)

½"

½"

20¹/₄"

19¹/₄"

½"

½"

½"

22

23

24

Use the pediment to transfer the arc onto the upper panel.

Side Rail and Molding
(Inside View)

6½"   3½"   4"   12¹/₈"

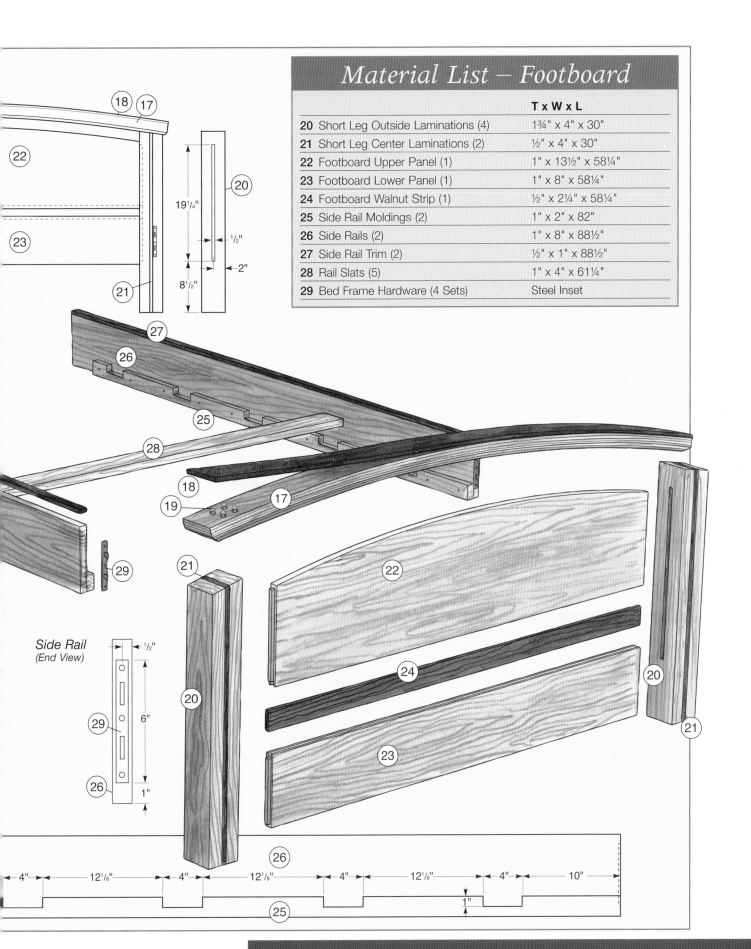

Material List – Footboard

		T x W x L
20	Short Leg Outside Laminations (4)	1¾" x 4" x 30"
21	Short Leg Center Laminations (2)	½" x 4" x 30"
22	Footboard Upper Panel (1)	1" x 13½" x 58¼"
23	Footboard Lower Panel (1)	1" x 8" x 58¼"
24	Footboard Walnut Strip (1)	½" x 2¼" x 58¼"
25	Side Rail Moldings (2)	1" x 2" x 82"
26	Side Rails (2)	1" x 8" x 88½"
27	Side Rail Trim (2)	½" x 1" x 88½"
28	Rail Slats (5)	1" x 4" x 61¼"
29	Bed Frame Hardware (4 Sets)	Steel Inset

Side Rail
(End View)

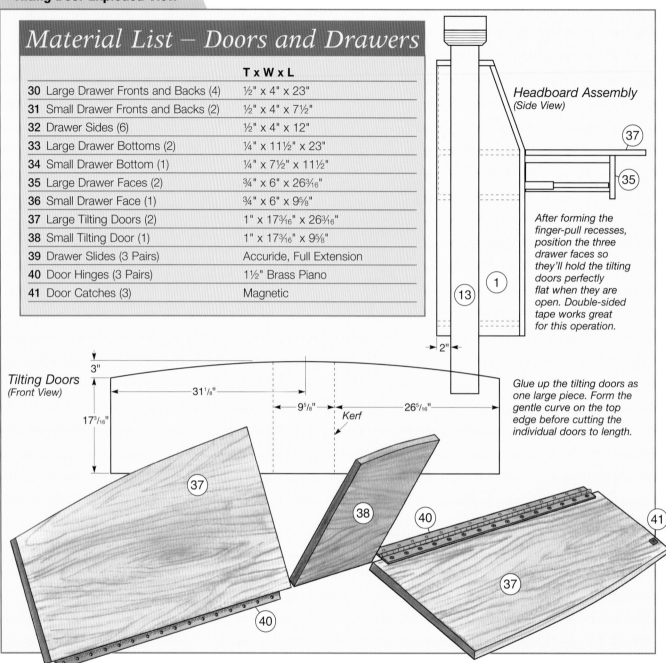

Material List – Doors and Drawers

		T x W x L
30	Large Drawer Fronts and Backs (4)	½" x 4" x 23"
31	Small Drawer Fronts and Backs (2)	½" x 4" x 7½"
32	Drawer Sides (6)	½" x 4" x 12"
33	Large Drawer Bottoms (2)	¼" x 11½" x 23"
34	Small Drawer Bottom (1)	¼" x 7½" x 11½"
35	Large Drawer Faces (2)	¾" x 6" x 26³⁄₁₆"
36	Small Drawer Face (1)	¾" x 6" x 9⅝"
37	Large Tilting Doors (2)	1" x 17³⁄₁₆" x 26³⁄₁₆"
38	Small Tilting Door (1)	1" x 17³⁄₁₆" x 9⅝"
39	Drawer Slides (3 Pairs)	Accuride, Full Extension
40	Door Hinges (3 Pairs)	1½" Brass Piano
41	Door Catches (3)	Magnetic

Headboard Assembly
(Side View)

After forming the finger-pull recesses, position the three drawer faces so they'll hold the tilting doors perfectly flat when they are open. Double-sided tape works great for this operation.

Tilting Doors
(Front View)

Glue up the tilting doors as one large piece. Form the gentle curve on the top edge before cutting the individual doors to length.

Figure 5: *Installing knockdown bed rail hardware in mortises keeps it invisible when assembled.*

Figure 6: *Heavy-duty drawer slides are an important feature because the drawers, when open, do double duty as door supports.*

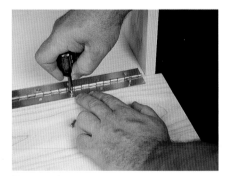

Figure 7: *Sewing-machine hinges were tested, but they weren't up to the job. Piano hinges offer the strength and support these doors need.*

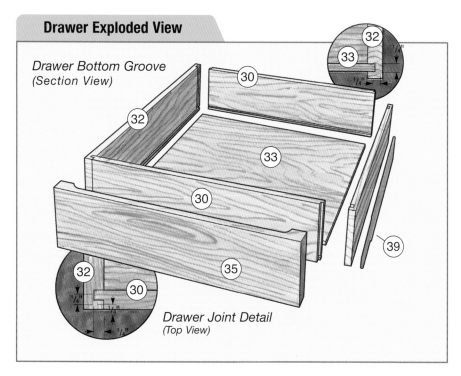

Drawer Exploded View

Drawer Bottom Groove
(Section View)

32

30

33

30

32

33

32

30

35

39

Drawer Joint Detail
(Top View)

¼" ¼" ¼"

¼" ¼"

exploded view, above. Next, mill a vertical dado in the drawer sides near each end on the same face as the drawer bottom groove. Each dado is ¼" square and located ¼" from the end.

Use the same ¼" router bit to cut rabbets on the ends of the drawer fronts to make a slick, locking corner joint. Dry fit the drawers together. When everything works, assemble the drawers with glue and clamps. Make sure they're flat and square.

Solid-Hardwood Drawer Faces

You'll give your bed a great look if you arrange a continuous grain pattern through the hardwood drawer faces (pieces 35 and 36) and the tilting doors above them (pieces 37 and 38). If you edge glue stock to produce this effect, match the grain along the joint so it looks as though all six parts were cut from the same board.

Following the manufacturer's instructions, use heavy-duty, full-extension drawer slides (pieces 39) to install the three drawers in their openings (see Figure 6). Full-extension slides allow the drawers to pull out far enough to support the doors above them. The heavy-duty rating means that even an unabridged edition of *War and Peace*

won't cause them to sag. Hold off on mounting the drawer faces until the doors are in place.

Uniquely Designed Tilting Doors

The three tilting doors in the headboard are what really fulfill a reader's dreams. All three conceal cavities large enough to store plenty of printed matter, while either of the larger doors drops down to become an instant desk (depending on which side of the bed you prefer). The smaller, middle door transforms into a shelf for popcorn or a remote control.

You have already glued up stock for the doors. Now, cut them to size. Rip and crosscut first, and then arch the tops on the band saw. Belt sand the saw marks away, and then sand all three doors and break their edges gently with 180-grit sandpaper.

Mount the doors using heavy-duty piano hinges (pieces 40), as shown in Figure 7. Mark the locations of the hinges on the doors and headboard. Install just a couple

of screws per hinge to ensure you have the alignment right. Once you're sure all is correct, install the remaining screws. When the doors fit nicely, mount the magnetic door catches (pieces 41) to keep the doors from accidentally opening. With all three drawers mounted in their openings and fully extended, open the tilting doors. Locate the drawer faces so they'll support the doors at a true 90°.

Use double-sided tape or hot-melt glue to temporarily locate and attach the drawer faces to make sure they're properly spaced left to right. Remove the drawers, and secure the faces with screws, working from inside the drawers. Predrill and countersink for your screws. When all the holes have been drilled, remove the faces, and use a ¾" core-box bit mounted in your router table to create the finger pulls. Clamp stops to the fence to keep the recesses spaced about 1" in from each end.

Final Touches and Finishing

The only thing left to do before you pull out the mattress and take a nap is to apply a finish. Remove the drawers, and sand everything down to 220 grit. Use a tack cloth to remove the dust, and apply a coat of clear sanding sealer. Follow this with three coats of satin polyurethane, sanding lightly between each coat with 400-grit wet/dry paper.

Maple and Padauk Bed Frame

Getting a look of sophistication can be simpler than you imagined. With its combination of two furniture styles, as well as two wood species, this bed frame has quite a bit of flair—but its distinctive lines were achieved using just basic joinery and one primary tool, the router.

by Chris Inman

Furniture projects generally fall into stylistic categories. There's Shaker, Scandinavian, country, and many other specific styles common to our woodworking repertoire. However, the design of this bed frame is quite unique: It's a hybrid that captures elements from two different styles. First, the overall design reflects strong influences from the Arts and Crafts period, particularly the designs of Frank Lloyd Wright. On the other hand, the bedposts are reminiscent of shapes frequently found on postmodern pieces. Of course, the bed can be made from any number of different woods, but the contrast of honey-colored maple with the deep blood red of padauk creates a striking combination.

It's a treat to build such an elegant piece of furniture, especially once you discover how uncomplicated the construction is. The primary joint in this bed frame is a basic mortise and tenon made almost entirely with a router. With the addition of a table saw and a few hand tools, you can readily make this bed.

The construction took about 40 hours, and the materials cost about $400. You'll need 16 linear feet of 3" x 3" maple for the posts, 30 board feet of 6/4 maple for the rails (milled to 1¼" thick), 8 board feet of ½"-thick padauk, and a small amount of ⅛"-thick padauk for the stripes in the posts and ball caps. There are a few other odds and ends in the Material List that you'll also need (see page 142). The bed rail fasteners and 3"-diameter wood balls are available from Rockler Woodworking and Hardware (800-279-4441, *www.rockler.com*).

I planed all of the material, and hefting that thick maple around got to be tiresome after 3 hours of work. Your alternative would be to have it milled at the lumberyard.

Cutting the Stock

When you get your planed material back from the lumberyard, begin ripping the major bed components to width. Rip the side rails (pieces 1) and lower rails (pieces 2) to a width of 7", and cut the upper rails (pieces 3) 3" wide. Rip the ½"-thick padauk into 1½"-wide slats

Figure 1: *Round over the edges on the padauk slats by raising the ¼" bit so the outside tip of its curve is even with the table surface. Align the face of the fence with the outside edge of the bit's bearing.*

(pieces 4 and 5), and cut a 24"-long piece of ¾"-thick padauk to a width of 5⅜" for the platforms (pieces 6) that sit on top of the four posts.

Before moving on, remember that all woods are toxic to varying degrees, and exotics can be especially toxic. Be sure to use a dust mask and to wear a long-sleeve shirt and possibly gloves, depending on how sensitive you are to the fine dust that is created and thus could be inhaled or contacted while working with these woods. Padauk, for instance, can be a skin irritant. If you have a dramatic reaction to working with a certain wood—and this is possible with any species—contact your doctor immediately.

Once you've ripped these pieces to width, crosscut them to the lengths shown in the Material List. The lower and upper rail lengths include enough material for 1¼"-long tenons at both ends. Cut your bedposts (pieces 7 and 8) to length at this time, too. Make sure your crosscuts are square, as this will greatly affect upcoming steps.

Working at the Router Table

The edges of the padauk slats are routed with a ¼" roundover bit, which creates a total roundover of ½" on the slat edges. The advantage of this technique is that the slats will fit perfectly in mortises routed with a ½"-diameter straight bit. Set up your router table with the ¼" roundover bit, and rout all the slat edges (see Figure 1). A small ridge will likely remain after routing the edges, so lightly sand the pieces to smooth the roundovers.

Replace the bit in the router table with a ⅜" roundover, and rout the edges on the platforms in a similar fashion, again sanding lightly to remove any ridges.

Now, switch to a ⅛"-diameter straight bit in your router, and set the fence 1½" from the bit's center. Raise the bit to a height of ³⁄₃₂", and rout a groove centered in the front and back of each of the four bedposts. Proceed slowly, because a ⅛" bit is somewhat fragile.

Before routing the mortises in the bedposts, rip the padauk inlay strips (pieces 9) to go into the grooves you just routed. Set your table saw blade to a height of ¼", and rip eight strips ⅛" wide. Normally, it isn't advisable to trap a narrow strip between the blade and the fence, but this material is so light and flexible that it's unlikely to shoot out of the saw as long as you maintain control of the stock. Rip the padauk to within a foot of its end, cutting the strips to fit the groove snugly, and then reach around and pull the last few inches through the blade. Run a small bead of glue in each of the post grooves, and press the inlay strips in place.

Routing Mortises

Routing the mortises in the upper and lower rails is tiring work. There are lots of cuts to make for all the slats, and it takes concentration to remove the material in the right places.

Figure 2: *Simplify the mortising process by making the jig shown here. The jig opening must be designed for your router to limit the length of cut to 1½". The edge guide rides against the jig while centering the bit on the 1¼"-thick rail stock. Align the centering mark on the jig with the center of each mortise.*

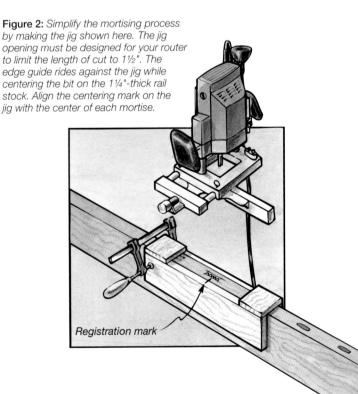

Registration mark

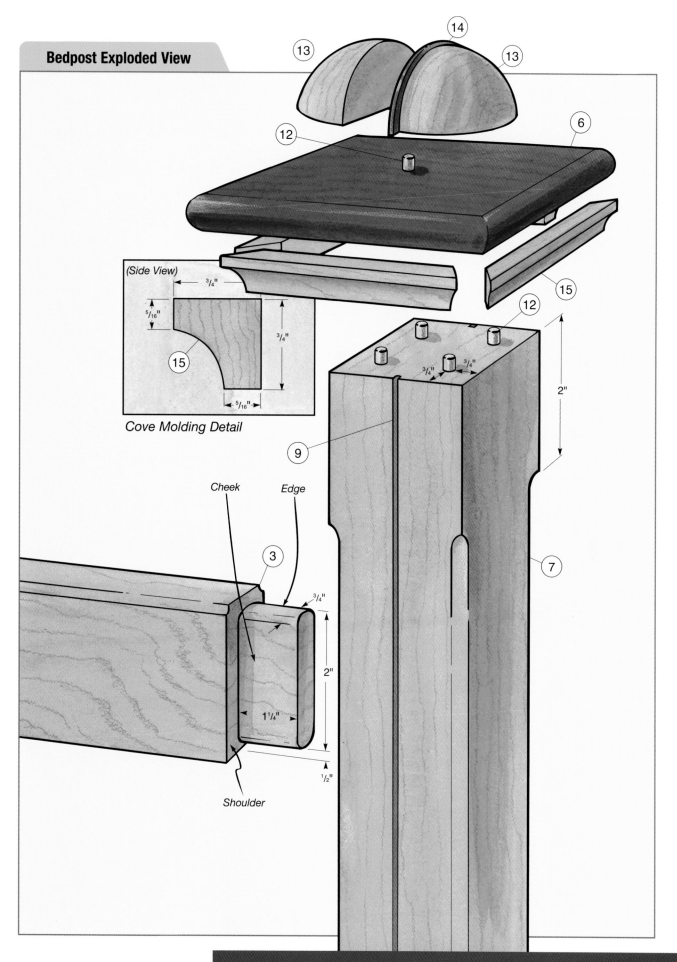

(13) (14) (13)

(6)

(12)

(Side View)

¾"

⁵⁄₁₆"

¾"

(15)

⁵⁄₁₆"

Cove Molding Detail

(12)

(15)

(9)

¾" ¾"

2"

Cheek   *Edge*

(3)

¾"

2"

(7)

1¼"

½"

Shoulder

To simplify the process, the first thing you need to do is make a jig that limits the length of cut to 1½". The jig I made from scrap plywood is simple and easy to set up (see Figure 2 on page 138); just be sure to alter the spacing between the stop blocks to accommodate the size of your router's base.

Lay out the slat mortises on the rails (see the drawings on page 142), and equip your router with a ½" straight bit. Adjust the router's edge guide to center the bit on the rail's edge. Line up the registration mark on the jig with the mortise location mark, and clamp the jig to the rail. Set the router on the edge of the rail between the jig stops, and plunge the bit into the stock to take a ¼"-deep pass, followed by a ½"-deep pass to complete the mortise. Continue this process until all the slat mortises are cut in the upper and lower rails.

Next, sand the padauk inlay strips flush with the bedposts, and then follow the drawings on page 142 to lay out the mortise locations in the posts. Precision really pays off here, so take your time and mark everything carefully.

Now, chuck a ¾"-diameter straight bit in your plunge router, and adjust the edge guide to center the bit on the 3"-wide post. Set the depth of cut to 1⁵⁄₁₆".

Select the best side of each post to face you when you stand at the footboard, which is the most frequent view of a bed from within the room. When routing identical pieces like the posts, make it a habit to rout them all with the guide riding against the same point of reference. For instance, always bear the edge guide against the outside face of the posts. That way, any slight variation will be the same from post to post. Now, take a number of increasingly deeper passes to rout two mortises in each post for the upper and lower rail tenons. You'll find that the

router is easy to control with the edge guide attached and that stops aren't necessary to control the length of cut.

Once the mortises for the rails have been cut, install a ⅝" straight bit in the router, and leave the edge guide set for routing the center of each post. Adjust the cutting depth to equal the thickness of the back plate of the bed rail fasteners (pieces 10), and rout these shallow mortises in the posts (see the exploded view at right). Finish this step by squaring the corners of the mortises with a chisel to fit the slotted piece of each pair of fasteners.

With a pencil, outline the slots that will engage the hooks on the other fastener piece, and exchange the ⅝" bit in your router for a ¼" straight bit. Now, rout ¼"-deep channels at these two locations within each mortise to accommodate the hooks on the mating fastener pieces.

Routing the Tenons

The upper and lower rails are really too long and heavy to handle on a table saw while cutting their tenons, so use a router to remove the cheek material, followed by a fine-cutting Japanese saw and a chisel to cut the shoulders (see the exploded view on page 139).

Use a ¾" straight bit in your router, and set the edge guide to limit the cut to 1¼" from the end of the rail to the outside edge of the bit. Lower the bit ¼", and pass the router over both sides of a piece of scrap to make sure the tenon fits the mortise. When you rout this way, don't define the shoulder with the first pass, but instead, work toward it and make the shoulder cut the last pass. Once you're satisfied that everything is correct, rout the cheeks for the eight rail tenons.

With a Japanese saw or other small, fine-toothed handsaw, cut the

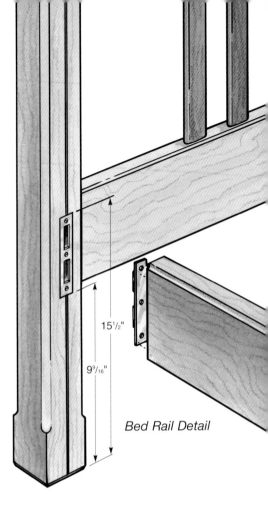

15½"

9⁹⁄₁₆"

Bed Rail Detail

edge shoulders on every tenon, and then pare the shoulders square with a sharp chisel. The last step in forming the tenons is rounding over the edges with a file so they fit into the router-cut mortises. Use a medium-toothed cabinetmaker's file to round the edge corners, and use a chisel to cut the small hump of wood that always remains at the inside corners of the shoulders after filing. Chamfer the leading edges of the tenons with the file so they slip into the mortises easily.

Post and Side Rail Details

Before assembling the headboard and footboard, take care of a few minor details on the bedposts while they're still easy to maneuver. The first thing to do is lay out four dowel holes on the top of each post (see the exploded view on page 139) for securing the padauk platforms. Mark the locations, and drill ¼" holes ⅝" deep using a portable drill. Now, insert ¼" dowel centers into the holes, and center the platforms on each post. When the platforms are positioned, press down on them to dent the wood with the dowel centers. Next, drill ¼" x ½"-deep holes at these locations. Don't glue the platforms to the posts until after assembling the headboard and footboard.

The four corners of the posts and the top edges of all the rails are routed with a cove bit. On the rails, this detail extends the entire length, but on the posts, the routing is stopped short of the ends. Lay out the stopping points on the posts (3" from the top and 2" from the bottom), and chuck a ½"-radius cove bit in your router. Set the bit to cut ¼" deep, and rout the edges of the posts, stopping when you reach the endpoint lines. Make your first pass a shallow one, and stop slightly short of the lines. On the second pass,

Figure 3: *Hold the side rail in a bench vise while routing the bed rail fastener mortises. Clamping a scrap board flush with the rail's end stabilizes your router during this cut (bottom). Remember, you also need to cut two deeper channels within the mortise with a ¼" bit so the fasteners lay flat (top).*

cut full depth and rout right to the line. Try to avoid lingering at the line, or you'll burn the wood—if this happens, fashion a round-tipped scraper to remove the burned wood. After the posts are done, rout the top edges of the rails from end to end.

Take care of one other small item by turning the posts upside down and routing a ³⁄₁₆" chamfer on their bottom edges. This makes the posts appear to be set off the floor a bit and prevents catching the wood and chipping the corners when the bed is moved.

The ends of the side rails are also mortised to accept the hooked bed rail fasteners. Once again, this is easily done with a router, an edge guide, and a ⅝" straight bit. Adjust the guide to center the bit on the edge of the

1¼"-thick rails, and set the depth of cut to equal the thickness of the back plate on the fasteners. Now, lay out the start and stop points on the ends of the rails. Clamp on a wide auxiliary board so it's flush with the end of the rail, and then plunge the bit into the stock and rout the mortise (see Figure 3). Do this to both ends of each rail, and then square the rounded ends of the mortises with a chisel. Now, set the fasteners in place, and give them a sharp blow with a hammer. When you remove the fasteners, you'll notice two separate indentations caused by the stamped hook retainers on back of the fasteners. Rout ¼" channels at these locations so the fasteners will sit all the way into the mortises, as shown in the inset photo in Figure 3.

Ledger Strip Placement

4³/₄"

¹/₂"

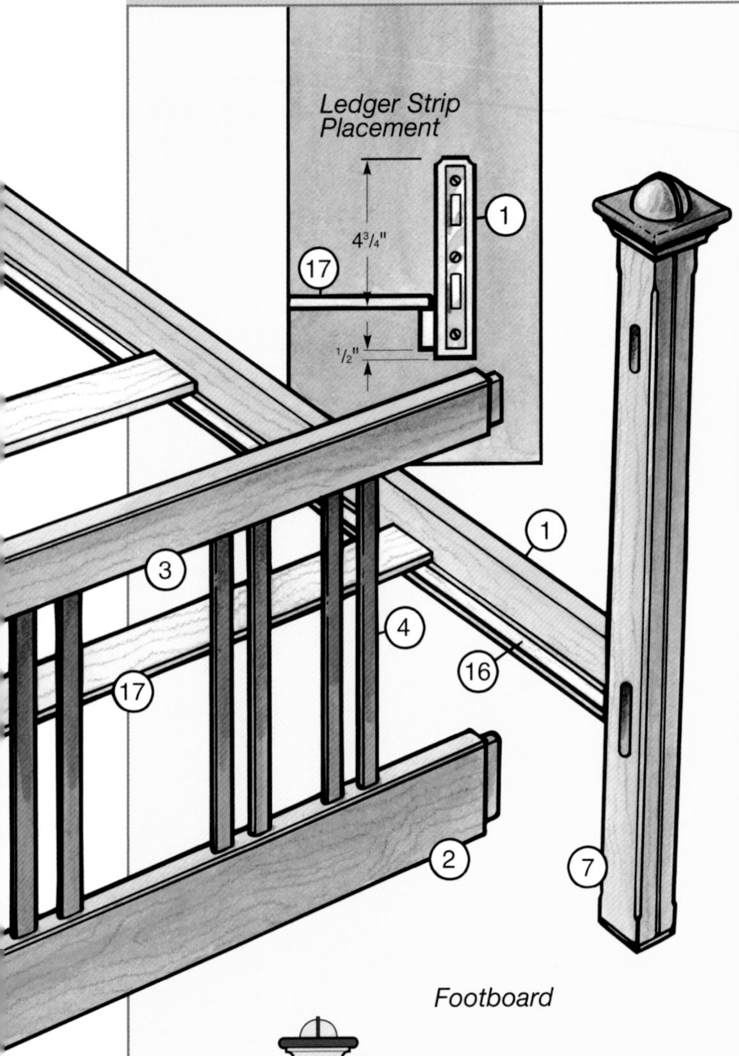

Material List

		T x W x L
1	Side Rails (2)	1¼" x 7" x 80"
2	Lower Rails (2)	1¼" x 7" x 62½"
3	Upper Rails (2)	1¼" x 3" x 62½"
4	Padauk Footboard Slats (12)	½" x 1½" x 22"
5	Padauk Headboard Slats (12)	½" x 1½" x 30"
6	Padauk Platforms (4)	¾" x 5⅜" x 5⅜"
7	Footboard Posts (2)	3" x 3" x 43¼"
8	Headboard Posts (2)	3" x 3" x 51¾"
9	Padauk Post Inlay Strips (8)	⅛" x ⅛" x 53"
10	Bed Rail Fasteners (1 Set)	6"
11	Bed Rail Screws (24)	#10-2"
12	Spiral Dowels (20)	¼" x 1"
13	Maple Balls (2)	3" Dia.
14	Padauk Ball Dividers (4)	⅛" x 1⅝" x 1⅝"
15	Cove Moldings (16)	¾" x ¾" x 6"
16	Ledger Strips (2)	¾" x 1¾" x 80"
17	Stretchers (4)	¾" x 3½" x 61½"

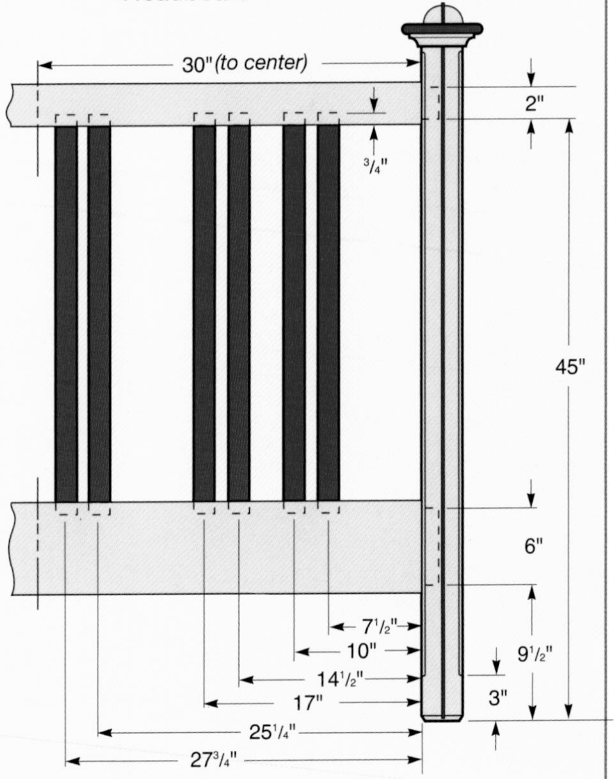

Footboard

30" (to center)

2"

³/₄"

37"

6"

9¹/₂"

3"

7¹/₂"

10"

14¹/₂"

17"

25¹/₄"

27³/₄"

Headboard

30" (to center)

2"

³/₄"

45"

6"

9¹/₂"

3"

7¹/₂"

10"

14¹/₂"

17"

25¹/₄"

27³/₄"

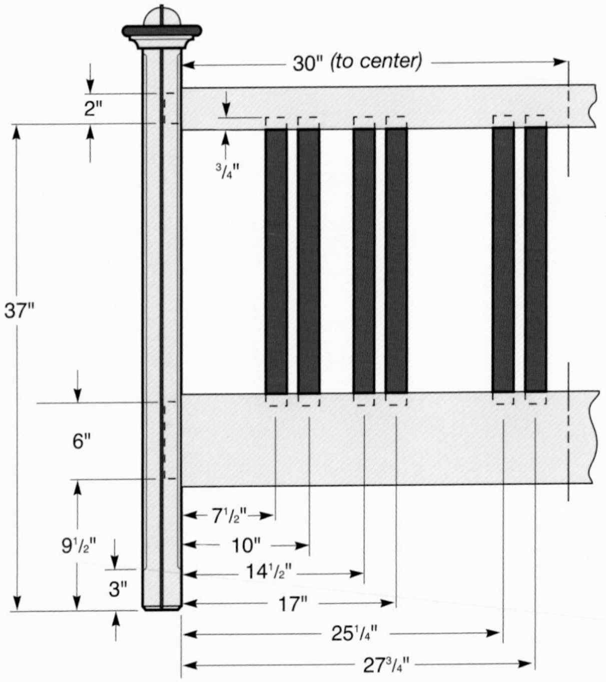

Set the fasteners into the mortises, and mark their screw hole locations. You might as well do this for the posts now, too. Drill 2"-deep pilot holes with a 5⁄32" bit, which should be just right for #10-2" flathead wood screws (pieces 11). However, don't install the fasteners until after the bed is finished.

Assembling the Headboard and Footboard

Before joining all the pieces in the headboard and footboard, sand everything to 150 grit. Be sure to ease all the edges on the maple, but don't lose the definition on the coved edges.

Organize all the parts for the footboard first, and be diligent about it. Once you've started putting glue in the mortises, you won't have time to go looking for a slat.

Padauk, due to its oily composition, sometimes fails to bond well with conventional glues. To overcome this problem,

Figure 4: *Use a V-jig for cutting the maple balls in half, making sure the ball fits very tightly. Cut slowly, and stop the saw when the blade exits the ball. Then, reach in and remove the two halves.*

QuickTip

Giant Band Clamps

Although bicycle inner tubes make great band clamps, sometimes even they are not big enough. Here's a science class trick that will double their size. Cut out a couple of inches to remove the valve, and then split the remainder lengthwise. Now, bring the ends together, twist one a half turn (180°), and apply 2" of tire-patching cement to join them. After the glue has dried, make another cut, and slice all the way around the circumference. When the cut returns to the starting point, you'll have one big rubber band, not two small ones, thanks to the twist you put in earlier.

Step 1

180° twist

Glue

Step 2

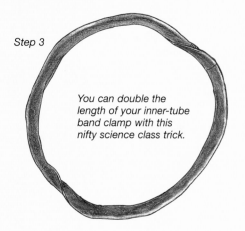

Step 3

You can double the length of your inner-tube band clamp with this nifty science class trick.

Figure 5: *A V-jig with only the top piece grooved is used for quartering the ball on a table saw. Once the ball is completely within the blade body, stop the saw so you can remove the quartered pieces.*

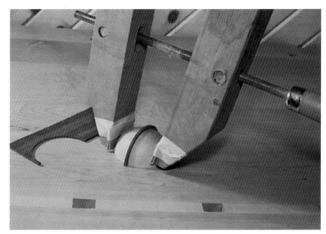

Figure 6: *A wooden hand-screw clamp works well to assemble the ball caps. Tape a folded piece of sandpaper to the ends of both jaws to get a better grip and to protect the maple ball sections.*

use epoxy. Begin spreading glue into all the slat mortises in the upper and lower rails and then inserting the slats into the lower rail. Now, pull the upper rail onto the other end of the slats, and spread glue in the post mortises and on the rail tenons. Pull the posts onto the rails, and check for squareness by measuring the diagonals. Use long bar clamps to hold everything together until the glue sets. At this time, glue the platforms onto the the footboard posts using ¼" x 1"-long dowels (pieces 12). Set the footboard assembly aside, and follow the same procedure for the headboard.

Making the Ball Caps

To safely cut the 3"-diameter maple balls (pieces 13), you must make a couple of simple V-jigs: one for cutting the balls in half on the band saw (see Figure 4 on page 143), and another for quartering them on the table saw (see Figure 5). Size each jig spacer so the balls are squeezed tightly.

Clamp a fence to your band saw table so the blade is centered on the V-jig, and push a ball into the jig with its end grain pointing right and left. Slowly

engage the blade and cut through the ball. Turn off the machine as soon as the blade exits the ball, and then reach in and remove the halves. Don't try pulling the jig back through the blade, as the tension on the ball will have closed the kerf and you'll just untrack the blade.

Now, cut each ball half into quarters using the table saw jig. Adjust the saw's fence to center the blade on the jig, and then proceed with the cut until the ball is just past the teeth and resting against the body of the blade. Stop the machine and remove the ball quarters from the jig. Again, don't try to back out of the cut or continue through the other side of the blade, because the teeth, which are wider than the blade body, will shave more material off the ball.

Next, cut out the dividers (pieces 14) that go between the quartered maple balls. Lay out two 3¼"-diameter circles on ⅛"-thick padauk, and draw a centerline through them. Now, cut out the circles, and then split them in half on a band saw.

Put glue on one face of each quartered ball, and align each pair with

a divider. I used a wooden hand-screw clamp with sandpaper folded and taped on the ends of the jaws to press the cap assemblies together (see Figure 6). The sandpaper helps keep the clamp from slipping. A band clamp would also work. Once the caps have been assembled, refine the edge of each divider on a drum sander, and then sand the cap. Use a belt sander to smooth the bottoms of the caps.

Use a center finder to position a dowel hole on the bottom of each of the four caps. You should also find the center of each post platform. Drill a ¼" x ½"-deep hole at each of these locations, and glue the caps to the platforms with a dowel (pieces 12).

Adding the Final Details

The next construction step is making the small cove moldings (pieces 15) that fit under the platforms. Use two pieces of ¾"-thick maple that are at least 3" wide and 24" long, and rout a ½"-radius cove on their long edges. Now, with the table saw fence set ¾" from the blade, rip the edges off the boards. Miter the strips to surround the top of the posts, and glue them in place, holding them to the platforms with spring clamps. You can use small brads if you're having trouble holding the molding with clamps.

The last detail on the bed frame is adding the ledger strips (pieces 16) along the inside of the side rails. Glue a 1¾"-wide strip ½" from the bottom of each rail. Once the glue has dried, cut the ends of the strips flush with the ends of the rails, and use a chisel to chamfer their sharp edges. Make four stretchers (pieces 17) to reach from rail to rail for supporting the box spring. Just use pine 1" x 4" material for these pieces, cutting them to fit between the rails while resting on the ledger strips.

Finishing Up

Sand everything through 220 grit before applying a finish. I applied Nordic Oil, a tung oil mixture that builds to a nice luster in three or four coats. Apply the first two coats with a brush, wiping off the excess each time about 15 minutes later. After the first two coats, sand the entire frame with 400-grit silicon carbide paper to remove any fine particles caught in the finish, and then apply another thin coat with a cotton rag. Add a fourth coat if you want more gloss.

You could use any other clear finish for this project if you prefer. Varnish, lacquer, or blond shellac would also highlight the grain and contrast.

Screw the bed rail hardware into their mortises, and mount the rails to the posts. Now, set the four stretchers so they span between the ledger strips, and drop in your box spring and mattress.

A good router is, without a doubt, the key tool required for constructing this bed frame. With the addition of a table saw, you can complete almost every step of the process, and the result, as you can see in Figure 7, is an elegant, sophisticated piece of furniture.

Figure 7: *A winning combination of geometric shapes and color contrast makes this bed appealing to see and to touch. Rugged maple construction ensures that it will stand the test of time, too.*

Pencil Post Bed

We spend more than a third of our lives sleeping—and many of us feel we could use even more sleep. Maybe you can't figure out a way to spend more time in bed, but you can make the time you do spend there … opulent. With that in mind, what could be more lavish than a beautiful handmade bed!

by LiLi Jackson

The pencil post design is one of the oldest American bed forms—dating back as far as 1690—so it has a wonderful sense of history. But the main reason I chose to build this Shaker-style piece is that I love its understated elegance. It fits with furnishings of nearly any decor or era, and this particular version can easily be knocked down, which is always a benefit with large pieces of furniture.

Getting Underway

After selecting an excellent stack of cherry lumber and milling it all to size, I glued the most highly figured boards together to create blanks for the posts and headboard (see the Material List on page 148 for their dimensions). After the glue had cured, I began laying out the posts (pieces 1). Starting from the bottom, I measured 12" up each post and marked a line dividing its width. From there, I measured up another 6" and drew a similar line. Then, using a square, I extended the lines completely around the post blanks. At the top and bottom

of each post blank, I marked points ⅝" in from each corner, and then I used a long straightedge to connect these points to the lines bisecting the post (see the post layout detail drawing on page 148). This describes the tapers on the posts. I repeated this process on the long face of each post blank to prepare for slicing the tapers.

I find it most pleasing to use a combination of power tools and hand tools on my projects. Often, I will use power tools at the beginning of the project to speed it up, and then end up by

using hand tools to get more of a feeling of precision. With the posts, I started my milling on the band saw. This is a very simple cut: You simply aim down the lines you just marked and start sawing. After cutting the first face, I taped the waste

Figure 1: *The first step in machining the pencil posts is done on the band saw. Slice off the tapered sections from the leg blank. Reserve the drop, and tape it back in place. Repeat the cut-and-tape process on successive faces of the post until you have cut all the tapers.*

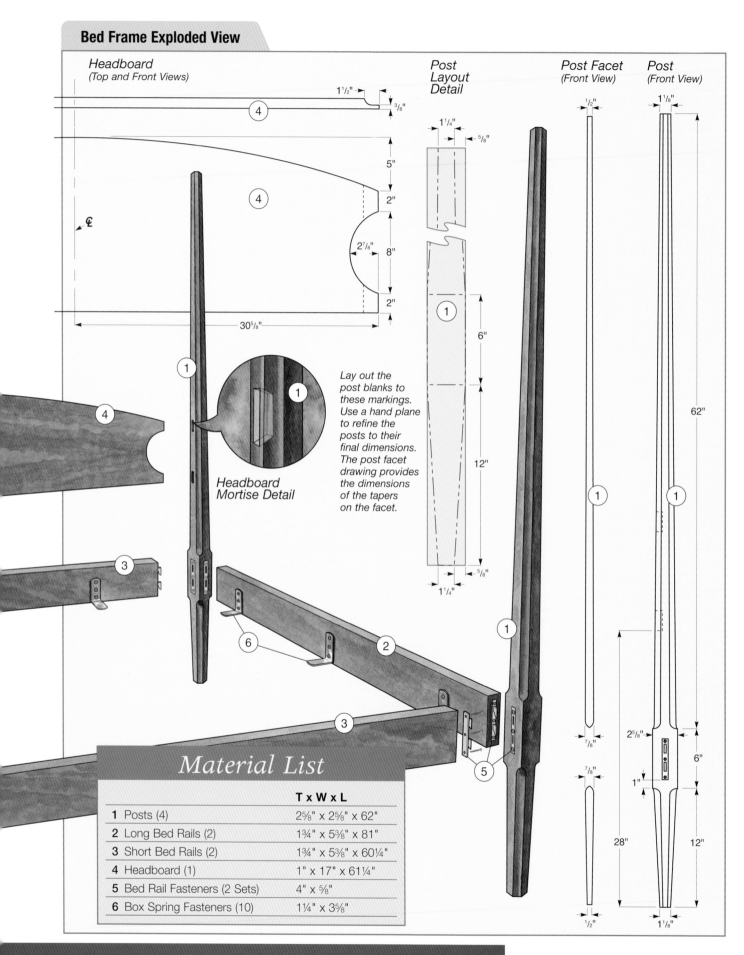

Bed Frame Exploded View

Headboard
(Top and Front Views)

1½"

³/₈"

5"

2"

2⁷/₈"

8"

2"

30⁵/₈"

Post Layout Detail

1¼"

⁵/₈"

6"

12"

⁵/₈"

1¼"

Post Facet
(Front View)

½"

⁷/₈"

⁷/₈"

½"

Post
(Front View)

1⅛"

62"

2⁵/₈"

6"

1"

28"

12"

1⅛"

Lay out the post blanks to these markings. Use a hand plane to refine the posts to their final dimensions. The post facet drawing provides the dimensions of the tapers on the facet.

Headboard Mortise Detail

Material List

		T x W x L
1 Posts (4)		2⁵/₈" x 2⁵/₈" x 62"
2 Long Bed Rails (2)		1¾" x 5⅜" x 81"
3 Short Bed Rails (2)		1¾" x 5⅜" x 60¼"
4 Headboard (1)		1" x 17" x 61¼"
5 Bed Rail Fasteners (2 Sets)		4" x ⅝"
6 Box Spring Fasteners (10)		1¼" x 3⅝"

back in position to recreate a flat surface to cut from (see Figure 1 on page 147). This is much like making the initial cuts on a cabriole leg.

After sawing the tapers on all four posts, I took the posts back to my workbench and smoothed out the tapers with a 04½ bench plane. Then, with the post held between bench dogs, I rotated it 45° and planed down each of the long edges to form the octagonal "pencil" shape. The wood I selected had a lot of figure to it, and consequently, the grain often ran in different directions. So I turned to a spokeshave (often cutting in the exact opposite direction as I was with the plane) to handle that wild grain. As is commonly seen on the pencil post design, I wanted the octagon to merge into a squared-up section where the bed rails (pieces 2 and 3) would join the posts. To achieve that shape, I used a Dremel rotary tool and my trusty spokeshave to merge the taper up into the squared-up rectangular post segment (see Figure 2). Take your time and form symmetrical curves—these small details add grace and elegance to this simple design.

Bed Rail Hardware

To connect the posts together, you need bed rails, and to link the bed rails and posts, you can use bed rail fasteners (pieces 5), as I did. To chop the two-level mortises for the hardware in the post, I used a mortising machine (see Figure 3 on page 150). Later, when I made the bed rails (ultrasimple rectangular shapes), I formed matching mortises using a couple of bench chisels. The only step remaining with the bed rails was to knock down their long edges so I wouldn't hurt myself while getting out of bed! I completed this with a roundover bit in my router table.

Figure 2: *Shaping the posts requires a series of steps combining both hand tools and power tools. After the initial tapers are removed on the band saw, additional facets are created using a plane and a spokeshave. The curved details that end the facets are carved with a rotary tool.*

4 1/8"

5/8" **1/2"**

Figure 4: *To attach the headboard, you'll need to create mortises in two of the bedposts. Make the mortises using a drill press with a ½" Forstner bit, and then clean them up with a sharp chisel.*

Figure 5: *A combination of careful layout and trial-and-error test fittings is required to fit the headboard tenons in their mortises. The bed rail hardware holds the bed together so firmly that you do not need to glue the headboard in place. Thus, the bed knocks all the way down to its nine pieces when it's time to move.*

Figure 3: *A mortising machine is just the ticket to form the two-step mortises on the posts. The segment of the bed where you mount the hardware remains sticked up (square and rectangular). This makes it much easier to chop the mortises. Alas, the mortises on the ends of the bed rails must be chopped the old-fashioned way, with a couple of sharp chisels.*

Technically, I now had a working bed, but what would a bed be without a headboard? Since I was going for that gracefully simple Shaker look, I drew out a rather traditional headboard shape. (It easily prevents my pillows from falling behind the bed.) Once again, I stepped over to the band saw to slice out the overall shape and then to the belt sander to remove the band saw marks. Look to the drawings on page 148 for all the construction details on the headboard (piece 4) and for details on shaping its tenons. I used a four-in-hand file to scoop out the backs of the tenons.

One of the most satisfying aspects of making furniture yourself is that you can design it to fit your needs. Depending on the height of your mattress and box spring—and the overall appearance you want the bed to have—you can locate the headboard to suit your needs. Back at the drill press, I chose two posts and mortised them for the headboard using a ½" Forstner bit, and then I cleaned up the mortises with a sharp chisel (see Figure 4). You will need to do some trial-and-error fitting with both the mortises and the headboard's tenons (see Figure 5).

Subtle Finishing Additive

Hooray! The bed is built. On to my absolutely favorite part: sanding and finishing (just kidding!). There is a lot of surface area to cover, but for environmental and traditional design reasons, I chose to brush on shellac. I prepared a batch of blond shellac mixed with some powdered mica and brushed it on with a good natural-bristle brush (see Figure 6). I sanded between coats with 320-grit sandpaper. One trick I used for shellacking the posts was tapping a small finish nail into each end of the posts. That way, you can rest the posts on the nails to create a rotisserie effect while you apply the finish. After four coats, I lightly buffed all of the pieces with steel wool, and then, still using steel wool, I rubbed on a coat of wax.

Have you ever heard the saying "Good night, sleep tight; don't let the bed bugs bite"? In olden days, people used to weave rope through the bed rails to create a surface for their mattress to lie on. Every so often, they would have to tighten the rope to keep the bed from sagging (hence, the sleep tight…oh, you got that). If you have a box spring to put your mattress on, you can get off easy by screwing in a few box spring fasteners (pieces 6) to each bed rail (although this will do nothing to prevent the bed bugs from biting).

This wasn't the hardest project I've ever built, but all that sanding sure left me needing a nap. Now that I've made my bed, I intend to sleep, perchance to dream up my next must-build project. If you intend to do the same, remember, as Goethe said: "Dream no small dreams for they have no power to move the hearts of men."

Figure 6: *I used blond shellac mixed with a small amount of powdered mica to add a subtle sparkle to this traditional finish.*

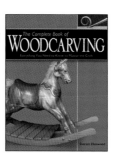
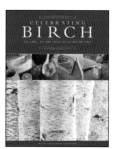

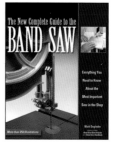